Technology

Fountainheads

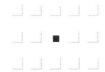

Technology Fountainheads

The Management

Challenge

of R&D

Consortia

■

E. Raymond Corey

Harvard Business School Press   Boston, Massachusetts

Library of Congress Cataloging-in-Publication Data

Corey, E. Raymond.
   Technology fountainheads : the management challenge of R&D
consortia / E. Raymond Corey.
      p.   cm.
   Includes index.
   ISBN 0-87584-723-4 (alk. paper)
   1. Research, Industrial—United States—Management.
   2. Research institutes—United States—Management.
   3. Consortia—United States—Management.   I. Title.
   T176.C597   1997
   658.5′7′0973—dc20   96-11016
                                                              CIP

The paper used in this publication meets the requirements of the American
National Standard for Permanence of Paper for Printed Library Materials
Z39.49-1984.

Dedication

This book is dedicated to the Honorable Joseph C. Swidler, chairman of the Federal Power Commission from 1961 to 1965, whose vision inspired the founding of the United States' first R&D consortium, the Electric Power Research Institute; and to Dr. Chauncey Starr, EPRI's first chief executive officer, who laid the foundations for a technology institute of enduring value to the electric power industry and to the nation.

Contents

Preface

Recently, having devoted my career to teaching and writing about for-profit businesses, I became interested in learning about the management challenges of nonprofit organizations. I chose to focus on R&D consortia. Such institutions have played an important role in European economic development, and have contributed significantly to Japan's rise in the world market for semiconductors, starting in 1976. R&D consortia began to emerge in the United States in 1973, with the founding of the Electric Power Research Institute. These collaborative ventures took as their mission the advance of technology in entire industries.

In a nation such as this, with an economy built on free market principles and competition, such a development seemed a departure from the tenets that have contributed to our high standard of living and our leadership role in world markets. A closer look, however, has persuaded me that the rise of R&D consortia in the United States signifies not the muting of interfirm rivalry, but progress toward a more sophisticated concept of global competition. It seems abundantly evident, too, that R&D collaboration among firms, with the government's participation, has accelerated market growth in the United States and added to our strength, if not supremacy, in global business competition.

R&D consortia interested me in another respect—that is, the particular challenges of managing such institutions. What I have learned is that the problems and requirements of effective consortium management differ significantly in degree from those of private enterprise, for three reasons. First, each consortium has a plethora of internal and external stakeholders to satisfy. Second, most are deeply involved with government agencies, ranging from state and federal regulatory agencies and administrative departments to the United States Congress. Third, unlike private enterprise, the owners of consortia are the clients. Taken together, these factors put constituency management at the very heart of the challenges confronting R&D consortia leadership.

Finally, I was curious about several other matters. What conditions have led to the rise of interfirm R&D collaboration at this particular time in our economic history? What roles do R&D consortia play in the context of a national technology research and development network comprised of university research centers, corporate laboratories, national labs, and for-profit research contractors? And how does the United States' experience with this relatively new form of enterprise compare with that of Europe and Japan?

I began, as I have always done in research, by writing case studies. In this instance, I selected six consortia that together covered a wide range in terms of membership size and revenue levels, industries served, and R&D sourcing modes. In particular, I chose some of the oldest consortia, on the hunch that I might learn more from their years of management experience. They include the Electric Power Research Institute (founded in 1973), the Gas Research Institute (1978), Semiconductor Research Corporation (1982), Microelectronics and Computer Technology Corporation (1982), Bell Communications Research (1983), and SEMATECH (1987). In all instances, the managers of these organizations were supportive of this project, and most cooperative in granting interviews with members of their management, in supplying file data, and in suggesting other sources of relevant information. My search broadened, then, to tap the experience and insights of government funders of U.S. R&D consortia and of member-company representatives. It included, as well, the examination of archival references to consortia in the United States as well as Europe and Japan.

I am persuaded that the emergence of R&D consortia as a relatively new form of enterprise is quite significant. In a world of rapidly advancing technology, R&D consortia play important roles in the development and dissemination of technology, in economic growth and environmental improvement, and indeed in global competition. I anticipate that these institutions will become increasingly important as we enter the next century. The challenge is to assure that they take on viable missions, are structured properly at the outset for their intended purposes, and are then managed effectively. It is in helping industry and government to cope with these challenges that I hope this book will make its contribution.

ACKNOWLEDGMENTS

I have had immense support from many sources. In particular, the Harvard Business School's Division of Research funded four years of travel, secretarial services, and other expenses of this study. Professor Richard E. Walton of the Harvard Business School has given me encouragement and guidance from the beginning. In addition, my book has benefited greatly from the comments and suggestions of Professors Joseph L. Badaracco and Richard E. Caves, also of the Harvard Business School.

The resources of the Harvard Business School's Baker Library have been invaluable; reference librarians Erika McCaffrey and Becky Smith could not have been more helpful in responding to my frequent requests for archival data. Jane M. Barrett, my secretary, has patiently worked through draft after draft of case material and numerous revisions of the manuscript. I am indeed indebted to her for her very willing and professional assistance in this undertaking.

Finally, I had the unstinting support of my wife, Charlotte W. Corey, who encouraged me every step of the way, lent an understanding ear, and gave me very helpful advice.

Technology

Fountainheads

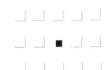

CHAPTER 1

SEMATECH'S Success

In a press release dated January 21, 1993, SEMATECH announced the breakthrough development of U.S.-made processing equipment capable of producing microscopic transistors with a line width of 0.35 microns, or approximately one three-hundredths the thickness of a human hair. This achievement significantly advanced the nation's state-of-the-art technology in the unremitting drive to make ever more powerful semiconductors through miniaturization.

The news bulletin noted:

> "When SEMATECH was created in 1987, we made a commitment to reestablish the U.S. semiconductor industry at the forefront of world manufacturing with the advent of 0.35-micron technology," said Bill George, chief operating officer for the Austin-based consortium.
>
> "By achieving that technology with all-U.S. tools, we have enhanced America's ability to compete in world markets—with exciting prospects for increased U.S. market share and domestic employment."
>
> "For SEMATECH," George added, "this means we have accomplished what we originally set out to do. For the American people, it means their $500 million investment in SEMATECH is paying off."

In 1980, the semiconductor manufacturing-equipment market equaled $888 million, and nine of the top ten makers of semiconductor manufacturing equipment were U.S. companies. By 1990 the market had grown to $4.1 billion, and five of the top six producers were Japanese. In terms of market share, the Japanese went from about 20 percent in 1980 to 45 percent in 1990, while the United States dropped from 80 percent to 42 percent.[1]

The nation's precipitous loss in market share in the semiconductor manufacturing-equipment sector alarmed both U.S. chip producers and the Department of Defense. If for any reason U.S. access to foreign equipment sources were to be cut off, the effect on one of the nation's most vital industries, as well as on the myriad commercial and military markets it served, could be devastating. The possibility was especially alarming given the fact that with technological advances, semiconductor manufacturing-equipment and chip design became obsolete about every three years. Also relevant were projections for the year 2000 that put the world market for semiconductor devices at over $200 billion, and the world market for electronics products at $2 trillion.[2]

By 1995, however, both U.S. makers of semiconductor manufacturing equipment and U.S. semiconductor fabricators had experienced a dramatic turnaround in their world market shares. The former went from an approximately 40 percent share in 1988 to an estimated 51 percent share in 1995. In that year, the world market for semiconductor manufacturing equipment amounted to $31 billion. U.S. semiconductor manufacturers, including companies such as IBM, Intel, Texas Instruments, and National Semiconductor, went from a 40 percent world market share in 1987, the year of SEMATECH's founding, to 46 percent of the 1995 world market, estimated at $152 billion. In each product category the United States was the world's leading producer (table 1.1), an achievement for which SEMATECH could take considerable credit. And in each category the United States was a net exporter, selling substantially more product than it consumed in its domestic market (table 1.2).[3]

A HISTORY OF SEMATECH

SEMATECH was formed in 1987 as a consortium of fourteen U.S. semiconductor manufacturers, with substantial funding from the Defense Advanced Research Projects Agency (DARPA) of the Department of Defense

TABLE 1.1 Estimated Market Shares by Region, 1995

	North America	Japan	Europe	Rest of World
Semiconductor Manufacturing Equipment	50.9%	42.0%	6.7%	0.3%
Semiconductors	46.16%	36.5%	7.49%	9.85%

Source: VLSI Research, Inc., San Jose, Calif., 1992.

TABLE 1.2   U.S. Production and Consumption of Semiconductor Manufacturing Equipment and Semiconductors, as a Percentage of World, 1994

	Consumption	Production
Semiconductor *Manufacturing Equipment*	33%	50%
Semiconductors	33%	43%

Source: VLSI Research, Inc., San Jose, Calif., 1992; Semiconductor Industry Association, *Semiconductors: Foundation for America's Future,* March 1992, Sec. A.

(DOD).[4] Its essential mission was to create a viable semiconductor manufacturing-equipment and materials industry in the United States, thus assuring that domestic chip producers would not be dependent on Japanese equipment sources. Envisioned as a research consortium in which both private corporations and the U.S. government would participate, SEMATECH paralleled comparable consortial arrangements in Japan. Industry initiatives came originally from panel discussions held in 1984 at the Semiconductor Research Corporation (SRC), a consortium formed earlier. Then, at the June 1986 board meeting of the Semiconductor Industry Association (SIA),[5] Charles Sporck, chairman of National Semiconductor (responding to the exhortations of George Scalise, chairman of an SIA public policy committee) volunteered to work with industry and government groups to define the need to strengthen U.S. competitiveness in semiconductors. Sporck's findings were presented to the SIA board that September. A task force was appointed to define the mission and recommend an organizational framework for an industry- and government-supported research consortium.

In the meantime, in December 1985, the deputy undersecretary of defense for research and engineering had requested that a task force of the Defense Science Board (DSB) be formed to assess the health of the U.S. semiconductor industry. The task force report, issued in February 1987, concluded that if current trends continued, the U.S. defense establishment would soon be dependent on foreign sources for state-of-the-art technology. The task force recommended "that the DOD should encourage and actively support with contract funding (approximately $200 million a year) the establishment of a U.S. Semiconductor Manufacturing Industry Institute formed as a consortium of U.S. manufacturers." (This wording is from a letter written to Charles Fowler, DSB chairman, by Norman Augustine, president and CEO of Martin Marietta. Augustine had been appointed to prepare the report, in which several other semiconductor industry executives also had a hand.)[6]

Defining a specific mission for SEMATECH came later, in response to an IBM study made public in 1986. It documented the rapid decline of the U.S. semiconductor manufacturing-equipment and materials industry, as domestic suppliers went out of business or were acquired by foreign corporations. Until then, it had not been clear what SEMATECH was being formed to do. Early discussions among SIA board members had considered but ruled out the possibility that SEMATECH might produce and sell semiconductors. Major companies, including IBM and AT&T, had been concerned about the antitrust implications of such a venture, as well as the possibility they would be obligated to purchase chips from SEMATECH. It was decided instead that the consortium would manufacture chips but not sell them, thus becoming a pilot plant for chip production.[7] Accordingly, the SEMATECH headquarters building in Austin, Texas, was designed as a manufacturing facility. But before construction was completed, SEMATECH'S mission was redefined as the rebuilding of a strong domestic manufacturing-equipment infrastructure.

Other factors were relevant in the delineation of a mission. Member companies regarded chip and manufacturing-process design as proprietary areas, in which each might seek to establish its own competitive edge. They felt SEMATECH should work at the "precompetitive" stage of the semiconductor value chain, extending from materials and manufacturing equipment to semiconductors to end products such as computers.

Larry Sumney, CEO of Semiconductor Research Corporation, recalls:

> It's safe to say that SEMATECH's mission came out of the IBM report showing that the semiconductor manufacturing-equipment industry had declined significantly. Originally, they [SEMATECH's founders] had intended to develop the technology for the next generation of ICs and a number of companies joined to get that technology: Harris, Micron Technology, LSI Logic. Those companies joined because they probably saw this as the lowest cost way that they could get these advanced processors. But there were intellectual property and competitiveness issues associated with that, and SEMATECH was left looking for what to do. Strengthening the semiconductor manufacturing-equipment industry turned out to be the answer.
>
> If you talk to the people who joined the consortium and then left, they would say it was because they signed up for one mission and then the mission changed.

They didn't feel that they could afford the membership if they weren't going to get what they had signed up for.[8]

In February 1987, Sporck, by then chairman of the SIA's steering committee on SEMATECH, led a lobbying effort in Washington to get government financial support. Also actively involved was Dr. Robert Noyce, cofounder and CEO of Intel, who testified at a congressional hearing as follows:

> We are asking that the government assume a role common for most of our major industrial rivals and which gives our competitors a large advantage. That is, to encourage the health and competitiveness of the most crucial and productive industries for national economic well-being. The advantage of this project is that government's role is temporary and the money is to be spent only on research (after the fifth year, SEMATECH would be funded only by its members). . . . To optimize the benefits of the funds we receive, we hope that the government will give maximum operational discretion to SEMATECH. The project will offer significant benefits to the nation as a whole. First, it will ensure the viability of the U.S. electronics industry . . . and second, it will maintain a domestic source of supply for the critical microelectronic products that are vital to our national defense.[9]

Three governmental studies were commissioned, one from the National Science Foundation, another from Congressional Research Services, and a third from the Congressional Budget Office. All favored the consortium initiative. In addition, numerous government departments were consulted, and the issue was widely debated in Congress. Federal legislation to approve government funding of SEMATECH was introduced on March 23, 1987, approved on December 18, 1987, and signed into law by President Reagan on December 22, 1987. It authorized an appropriation of $100 million for SEMATECH in fiscal year 1988, with the anticipation of continued government funding at that level in each of the following four years.

For six months after SEMATECH's founding, Larry Sumney, CEO of Semiconductor Research Corporation, served as the new consortium's interim head until a search committee chaired by Noyce could identify a permanent CEO. The search took longer than expected. Ultimately Noyce himself accepted the SEMATECH presidency, despite his saying earlier that he was too old for the job.

SEMATECH's first CEO was eminently qualified to be a consortium leader. He had cofounded two highly successful semiconductor manufacturing ventures, National Semiconductor and Intel, and was a founding member of the Semiconductor Industry Association. His widespread reputation in both industry and government circles helped to gain the support of government bodies and to secure DOD funding. In style Noyce was mild mannered and inspirational. He believed strongly in teamwork, delegation of responsibility, and operating through informal networks. Sumney credits Noyce with quickly setting the consortium's direction:

> In a reasonably short period of time he focused on the infrastructure issues, and that was precisely the right thing to do. He sorted through everything that had been said and all the directions that had been proposed and picked the one thing [strengthening the U.S. semiconductor manufacturing-equipment sector] to which SEMATECH could make a real contribution.[10]

Revered in the semiconductor industry, Noyce attracted exceptional talent on loan from member companies—people who wanted the opportunity to work under a leading scientist and cofounder of the semiconductor industry's most successful startup venture.

SEMATECH was planned as a five-year venture that would require an estimated $1 billion for R&D expenditures over its life. Funding would come through membership fees, set at 1 percent of each member's semiconductor sales revenue or semiconductor purchases, plus DARPA contributions of $100 million annually for five years. Membership dues for any one firm are now capped at $15 million; the minimum annual fee is $1 million.

Effect of SEMATECH on the Semiconductor Equipment-Manufacturing Industry

Unlike the semiconductor industry which is highly concentrated, the equipment-manufacturing industry is quite fragmented, and as of 1987, its numbers were declining. Many U.S. firms had been acquired by foreign companies, had merged with other domestic firms, or had gone out of business. Of the 130 domestic tool suppliers, 25 had sales of $10 million to $25 million; 60 had sales under $5 million. Each tended to specialize in one or two products.

Profits in this segment of the electronics industry are marginal, due in large part to the need for heavy expenditures on equipment improvement and development. Semiconductor manufacturing equipment becomes obsolete on a three-year cycle. Investment risks are great, and equipment development costs often exceed a company's net worth. In addition, the chance of timing new product development to coincide with a window of opportunity, when customers are building new plants or upgrading existing ones, is slim at best. Furthermore, customers need time to test new equipment; initially, they might order only one unit. Orders for more units might or might not follow a year later. The rewards can be diminished, as well, if the innovator does not have the capacity to meet volume demand when it comes. All these drawbacks—high development costs, the risk of failure, poor timing of new product introductions, lags in market acceptance, and limits on production capacity—when imposed on a fragmented industry, make it a fragile link in the U.S. electronics chain.

With the decline of the domestic equipment industry, U.S. chip manufacturers had come to rely increasingly on Japanese sources, which had developed a reputation for making reliable state-of-the-art equipment and for having market staying power. Because chip makers tend to standardize on one brand in each equipment category, domestic manufacturers were at a disadvantage in becoming suppliers of choice for both U.S. and foreign semiconductor producers.

Through SEMATECH, stronger, more efficient linkages have been forged between semiconductor producers and makers of semiconductor manufacturing equipment—between a highly concentrated industry and its fragmented and fragile supply infrastructure. One vehicle for coordinating product development programs at these two levels of the electronics industry value chain is the SIA-sponsored National Technology Roadmap for Semiconductors, a document prepared in 1991 by more than a hundred representatives of the semiconductor industry, government agencies, and the academic community, and updated in 1993. The Roadmap establishes agreed-upon industry technical goals for semiconductor performance specifications to the year 2010, and defines the technical developments needed to achieve those goals for the entire U.S. semiconductor industry. It also spells out the performance requirements for semiconductor manufacturing processes, equipment, and materials. The objective is to design and manufacture a one-gigabit SRAM (static random access memory) by the end of the decade.

SEMATECH has also made important contributions to the improvement of buyer-seller transaction processes. Working with SEMI/SEMATECH, an association of U.S. semiconductor equipment and materials manufacturers, SEMATECH provides annual information on the direction of technological development one to five years hence, and the pursuant priorities for next-generation manufacturing equipment and materials.

Other contributions come under the rubric of cost avoidance. One example is the work SEMATECH does in qualifying new tools, which saves its eleven member companies from having to conduct tests of their own. Another example is the development of a standard audit for qualifying suppliers, accepted by all SEMATECH member companies. Supplier qualification was once a long and costly procedure both for equipment manufacturers and their customers, and each purchasing department of a member company had its own idiosyncratic routine.

As of 1994, SEMATECH's total annual funding of $180 million—half from ARPA, DARPA's successor organization—was being used to support development projects with semiconductor equipment-manufacturing firms and the semiconductor-related work by university research centers. By 1995 SEMATECH employed over 800 people, 220 of them (about 60 percent of SEMATECH's technical staff) on temporary assignment from their member companies.

SEMATECH is currently confronted with a potentially substantial decline in funding, following its board's decision that after 1996 it will rely solely on member payments—thus voluntarily forgoing the $90 million a year contribution from ARPA. By 1996 ARPA will have provided half of SEMATECH's R&D budget over the first nine years of its existence. Member companies are presently discussing the extent to which SEMATECH might be required to reduce its workforce and cut its programs. Other issues under consideration are where to find new sources of revenue and whether to open up membership to other firms, including foreign companies—an action that would have to be predicated on a fundamental change of mission.

In the meantime, SEMATECH can take credit for playing a major role in developing successive generations of chip-making technology. It has helped to strengthen U.S. equipment builders and semiconductor manufacturers in international competition, and to protect the national interest in assuring the viability of a strong domestic industry at all levels. It has also helped to forge closer ties among equipment builders, semiconductor manufacturers, and electronics end-product producers. The result is greater integration in technology planning, reduced transaction costs, and lower levels of risk in the manufacturing equipment segment of the electronics value chain.

Reasons for SEMATECH's Success

What accounts for SEMATECH's success? First is its viable, sustainable, and nationally important mission. The restoration of a strong semiconductor manufacturing-equipment sector was critical to domestic chip manufacturers, and had significant ramifications for national defense and economic development. Second, SEMATECH works at a precompetitive level. Corporations such as IBM, Intel, and National Semiconductor can come together around a common problem without trespassing on those technology competencies that undergird each company's competitive advantage.

A third factor has been outstanding leadership. Noyce worked effectively to build constituency support among relevant government agencies, Congress, and the semiconductor industry. His reputation as an industry leader enabled SEMATECH to attract highly qualified technologists from member firms for two- to three-year assignments at consortium headquarters in Austin, Texas. This is a key factor both in planning and carrying out an R&D program and in transferring the technology to member companies' engineering and production personnel.

Fourth, SEMATECH secured government funding—$100 million a year for the first five years, and $90 million a year in 1993 through 1996—to cover half its operating budget. Such funding was important financially, and served as well to endorse SEMATECH's mission among member firms and government and industry constituents. As Noyce had requested, the government gave SEMATECH "maximum operational discretion." ARPA representatives monitored the consortium's progress closely, but did not seek to exercise administrative oversight or to become directly involved in policy formulation, R&D planning, or governance.

Fifth, SEMATECH is an industry-led initiative which has attracted firms accounting for 80 percent of U.S. semiconductor manufacturing capacity. Its membership represents the entire semiconductor manufacturing industry, and includes major semiconductor users as well.

Not unlike other ongoing consortia, however, SEMATECH must confront change. In this case, both its success and its loss of government funding after 1996 will force a review of its basic mission and its exclusive membership policies.

WHAT THIS BOOK IS ABOUT

SEMATECH is one of six R&D consortia to which this study gives particular attention. Taken together, they provide an experiential base for developing some of the themes introduced in the SEMATECH case: the need to translate some initial vision or purpose into a viable mission; the criticality of effective leadership; the need for support from all relevant constituencies; and the definition of a constructive government-consortium relationship at the outset.

These and other managerially oriented topics are the primary focus of this book; they are micro-level matters. At a micro, or managerial, level, the focus is on the factors that make for success and sustainability in the formation of consortia. These have to do with mission, leadership, membership policy, governance structure, R&D planning processes, and the strategy for sourcing and delivering R&D products.

This study does not attempt to assess consortia performance. Cost-benefit measures based on the economic value of consortia R&D to member companies and the nation cannot be calculated, because these consortia operate in a confluence of many streams of scientific endeavor: academic, corporate, government, and collaborative. In addition, the benefits of many, if not most, of the consortia's technical advances are not quantifiable. Rather, the relevant measures of consortia performance are qualitative and subjective. Has the consortium created value for its members, in terms of operational efficiencies, the development of a supply infrastructure, and/or the growth of end-product markets? Has the consortium effectively addressed the technical aspects of industry-wide issues, e.g., establishing product and service standards and improving environmental health and safety? Has it strengthened the industry in global competition? In the free-market competition for R&D funding, has the consortium grown in size and scope? Has it survived and adapted to the ever-changing competitive milieu, evolving member needs, advancing technology, and shifting political climate? Such judgments may be made only by consortia directors, members, other funders, and their several external constituencies.

At a macro level, this book considers the economic implications of the rise of R&D consortia as economic institutions. It describes what R&D consortia are and what they do and then identifies the conditions that have fostered their growth in this and other industrialized countries. Going beyond, this study considers their role in a national R&D sourcing system and their potential contribution to industrial development and national competitiveness. I also speculate on the effect of consortia on industrial organization, in particular, oligopolistic industry structures. Finally, I speculate on their future. Will they grow in importance and in contribution, or can we expect a decline in R&D consortia and their contributions to the advance of technology?

Finally, I probe the data generated through field research to assess what they might contribute to a theory of collective action. Existing theory draws on the experiences of public interest groups, lobbying organizations, national alliances, and communal groups. If we expand that context to include R&D consortia, to what extent might the theory be advanced?

The discussion that follows in this and subsequent chapters draws largely on case studies of six of the oldest continuing R&D consortia in the United States, including SEMATECH. The cases were developed through field interviews with managers and members in the six organizations, which are described briefly later in this chapter. Examples of other consortia are drawn from telephone interviews with their managers and from the public press and business media. Interviews with government funders provide a national-interest perspective. The chapters on the economic implications and theories of collective action draw both on these sources and on the academic literature.

WHAT ARE R&D CONSORTIA?

Like churches and country clubs, R&D consortia are self-governing, usually nonprofit organizations run for the benefit of their members. The owners are the customers, and their purpose is to develop new technology and put it into practice. Funded largely by member companies, with additional support often from government sources, they are vehicles for R&D cost-sharing in areas of common interest. They may be defined in terms of their membership policies, the nature of their R&D missions, their intended duration, and their R&D sourcing modes.

Classification of R&D Consortia

As for the first, an R&D consortium may have an open-membership policy, admitting any organization able to pay whatever fees may be charged and willing to participate in carrying out the group's mission. The Electric Power Research Institute (EPRI), with over seven hundred members, is one such organization. Alternatively, membership may be exclusive, in the sense that it is not open to certain classes of potential members—e.g., foreign companies. SEMATECH would fall into this category, in the sense that its membership is limited to U.S. firms only. A third category is the closed consortium, an R&D partnership that typically has a small number of members and is limited to specific firms. Bell Communications Research

(Bellcore), owned by the seven regional Bell operating companies (RBOCs), is a closed alliance.

Some consortia are structured horizontally to include firms at only one level of the industry. Others are organized vertically to bring together firms at different levels, often those that relate to each other as buyers and sellers.

With regard to the R&D mission, consortia may have as their purpose the development of R&D products in one or more of three broad categories: collective, selective, and proprietary. *Collective products* are technologies intended for general use, the benefits of which cannot be denied to any party, whether or not it is a consortium member. An example would be R&D products developed to cope with environmental problems such as smog, water contamination, and public safety. *Selective products* are those intended specifically for the benefit of member companies, such as technical training for company personnel and advanced operational technology. While such products may leak out to nonmembers through industry channels, their value may be discounted by the time lag between their initial development and their accessibility to nonmembers. By comparison, the development of *proprietary products* is intended to accrue solely to the advantage of those funding the research. That is, R&D consortia will often undertake customized projects for one member or membership subset, the purpose of which is usually the development of proprietary knowledge to benefit only project participants.

This suggests another dimension on which to classify consortia, *ongoing* versus *temporal.* Temporal endeavors are those that undertake some specific task and fold when the mission is completed or aborted. In contrast, ongoing consortia—for example, SEMATECH and EPRI—typically take on broad and evolving R&D agendas.

Finally, consortia may be described in terms of their R&D sourcing modes, which may be internal, external, or member-company personnel. Some, such as Bellcore, have large internal technology-development staffs. Others—SEMATECH and EPRI, for example—rely primarily on R&D outsourcing.

For purposes of this study, it will be useful to distinguish between *R&D consortia* and *R&D joint ventures,* or *alliances.* The difference is primarily one of purpose. Consortia work on noncompetitive R&D, including both collective and selective products. R&D joint ventures (alliances) are formed to develop technology that will lead to member firms' competitive advantage. Typically, joint ventures are closed partnerships with a limited number of members—say, two to six—focused on achieving some particular development objective. They are temporal, and tend to rely on the pooling of complementary member-firm assets to carry out their missions.

Though this book focuses on R&D consortia, particularly those that have broad agendas and are ongoing, examples of joint ventures are cited in discussions of corporate technology sourcing strategies and the appropriability of intellectual property.

Functions of R&D Consortia

Taken together, R&D consortia in the United States provide a broad range of products and services—broader, it would seem, than those of its counterpart organizations in Europe and Japan. They fall into these categories:

- development and dissemination of new industrial process technologies
- technical education and training
- environmental research (health and safety)
- supply-industry infrastructure development
- academic research and graduate education support
- end-product development and commercialization
- industry standard-setting
- industry disaster and crisis response

Industrial Process Technology. Over the last two decades, R&D consortia in the United States have made major contributions to the efficiency of member companies' operating systems, through which products and services are manufactured and delivered. They have been veritable fountainheads of new industrial process technologies.

Bellcore, a consortium of the seven RBOCs, developed SONET, a transmission standard for fiber-optic systems. Adopted internationally, SONET has made a fundamental change in the way telephone companies plan, operate, and maintain their networks. It has vastly increased transmission speed, line capacity, and service quality, at a lower operating and maintenance cost compared with copper-wire systems.

The EPRI has funded the development of new technologies for generating electricity through wind and solar power. In late 1994 it announced the development of a solar cell twice as efficient as existing cell designs in capturing power from the sun. The cell and its associated systems convert to electricity more than 20 percent of the solar energy that hits them, generating electric power at a cost of 5 to 6 cents per kilowatt hour. Financed by EPRI, the technology was developed at Amonix, Inc., a maker of solar energy systems based in Torrance, California.

Technical Education. The education of member-company personnel is an ongoing function of R&D consortia. Educational media include technical bulletins, conferences, task force meetings, and one-on-one sessions for member-company representatives and consortia personnel. Semiconductor Research Corporation (SRC), for example, received and distributed to its sixty-one member organizations over seventeen thousand copies of each of more than one thousand reports received from faculty and student recipients of SRC research grants in 1995. These were preprints of research papers submitted by SRC-supported faculty and student researchers in the form of journal articles, dissertations, and conference proceedings and presentations. A current initiative is the development of an Electronic Document Library, on CD/ROM, for the transmission of SRC research publications to company libraries, information centers, and individuals. The system allows the receiver to review document briefs, scan entire reports, and identify other works on the same subject and/or by the same researcher. For recruiting purposes, readers may access authors' resumes. SRC also conducted 88 technical meetings in 1995, with a total attendance of almost four thousand representatives of member companies, government agencies, and the academic community.

Bellcore, in addition to providing technical data to personnel in the seven RBOCs through bulletins and conferences, offers information services covering regulatory matters, accounting methods, and billing system design, among other topics.

EPRI holds conferences and task-force meetings and generates a steady stream of bulletins, reaching operating personnel in member companies at all levels. At Boston Edison, for example, more than three hundred employees are on EPRI's mailing list for briefs on technical advances of relevance to their work. They can access EPRI documents and confer directly with EPRI project managers and others through EPRINET, a computerized network linked to an E-mail system.

Environmental Research. One example is a consortium formed in 1994 by Du Pont, Monsanto, General Electric, Ciba-Geigy, Dow Chemical, and Zeneca. Its mission is to develop soil remediation processes to accelerate the in-situ biodegradation of chlorinated solvents. The project, scheduled to run for four years, will be funded for $12 million, with part of that amount coming from government agencies. A year before this initiative was taken, a consortium was formed by Monsanto, Du Pont, and General Electric to develop technologies for treating clay soils in situ. Of the $1.6 million budgeted for the project, $1.3 million comes from the Environmental Protection Agency and the Department of Energy. Both consortia originated through discussions of the EPA's Remediation Technology Development forum, which brings together representatives from industry and a range of federal government agencies.[11]

Environmental issues such as emissions control, energy conservation, and soil remediation may be addressed effectively at the industry level. No one firm is likely either to possess the resources for undertaking such massive efforts or to be willing to undertake them alone. Since the returns to the individual firm come in the form of meeting environmental standards and of saving costs, the funding of such research has a significantly lower impact on each firm's cost when the investment is shared.

Infrastructure Development. Many R&D consortia have been effective in building industry supply infrastructures. As noted, SEMATECH has significantly strengthened the U.S. semiconductor materials and equipment-manufacturing industry as a critical national resource. Working with the many small U.S. suppliers of semiconductor manufacturing-equipment, SEMATECH played a major role in reversing the nation's decline in that sector, bringing the U.S. share of the world market up from a low of 40 percent in 1988 to an estimated 51 percent in 1995.[12]

By funding academic research, SRC has helped to increase dramatically the university-faculty and graduate-student resources devoted to the development of silicon-based semiconductor technology. SRC channels funds from its member companies and participating U.S. government agencies to universities, for use in research and graduate training in semiconductor design and manufacture. By pooling funds for academic research, consortia members gain the benefits of a rationalized academic research funding program, avoid duplicative efforts, and save on the cost of administering their own programs for funding academic research and graduate training.

On the occasion of SRC's tenth anniversary in 1992, Professor Ken Wise of the College of Engineering at the University of Michigan observed:

The difference between this laboratory now and this laboratory in 1983 is 15 doctoral students versus 100, first of all. Now in terms of our ability to get those graduate students and to get the best graduate students, you need funding, you need interesting projects. I believe that the interaction with industry, the ability to be in a program where you've got industrial mentors that you can deal with, that help you work on real world problems; those have all been attractions. We've had very good luck in getting very good students. I won't claim that it was all due to SRC, but I think SRC had a very pivotal role back in the early '80s for the growth of everything that's come since.[13]

End-Product Development and Commercialization. Some consortia have contributed importantly to the development of new products and markets. In 1994, for example, Bellcore announced the development of a thin-film plastic battery half the weight of a nickel-cadmium battery and a third the weight of a lead-acid battery, but with equal power and a significantly lower rate of deterioration in storage. Its flexible form and light weight make possible new designs for portable electronic devices as well as other, completely new battery-powered products.

Contributing to member-company revenue growth, EPRI developed heat pumps for residential and commercial heating and cooling that were 30 percent more efficient than conventional models and surpassed gas furnaces in overall systems efficiency. At the Gas Research Institute (GRI), an early success was the pulse combustion furnace (1980). Developed in cooperation with Lennox and the American Gas Association laboratories, it promises an efficiency rating of 90 percent or more, compared to 50 to 60 percent for conventional gas furnaces. All U.S. gas furnace manufacturers now offer units based on pulse-combustion technology.

Not just market growth per se, but growth in *industry* market share may be a consortium objective. Thus end-product development programs at GRI and EPRI help the gas industry and electric power utilities, respectively, to compete for a larger share of the domestic energy market.

Industry Standard-Setting. Because their memberships often represent a high percentage of total industry output, some R&D consortia have taken on a central role in national and international standard-setting. In the information-technology industries, in particular, standard-setting has become increasingly important with the rise of open systems—a computing philosophy that allows the interworking of and/or substitution for any component of a system. Thus, to participate in information-technology markets, vendors need commonly accepted standards in order to achieve interoperability. Traditionally, de facto standards have been set by major industry players such as IBM and AT&T. But an accelerating rate of technological change and truncated product life-cycles are making it increasingly costly for any one vendor to risk unilateral standard-setting in a gamble that the industry will follow. Instead, companies see consortia as the logical institutions for establishing standards to which all will adhere.[14] The consortium, CAD Framework Initiative, established in 1988, develops interoperability standards for computer-aided design. Its budget is less than $2 million, a third of which comes from the federal and state governments. Its forty members represent an estimated 90 percent of the worldwide computer, telecommunications, aerospace, and semiconductor industries combined. The results of its work are disseminated largely through commercial software vendors.

Disaster and Crisis Response. Finally, some consortia have developed crisis-response capabilities. At Bellcore, for example, one mission of the research group in chemical and material sciences is to study the effects of fire, flood, dust, acid, and other contaminants on telephone equipment; to investigate ways to detect impending disasters; and to be on call to assist when disaster occurs. Thus, when Ameritech's Hinsdale, Illinois, central office caught fire on May 8, 1988, shutting down forty thousand telephone lines, including those at O'Hare International Airport, Bellcore representatives were on the scene shortly thereafter to assess the damage and prescribe remedial measures.

SIX THAT LED THE WAY

The six consortia chosen for this study were selected to cut across the parameters just described, with the exception that all are ongoing. Because they are among the oldest consortia in this country, they offer opportunities to learn from their long experience. Three draw their members from regulated industries—electric power, natural gas, and telecommunications—and three others from the more intensely competitive semiconductor industry, which permits comparative analysis both across and within those two categories. Other dimensions along which they may be usefully compared include size: the six range in membership from just seven to more than seven hundred, and in annual budgets from $25 million to approximately $1 billion.

In addition to SEMATECH, the five consortia that are the primary focus of this study are the Semiconductor Research Corporation (SRC), Microelectronics and Computer Technology Corporation (MCC), the Electric Power Research Institute (EPRI), the Gas Research Institute (GRI), and Bell Communications Research (Bellcore).

Table 1.3 provides selected current data profiling these six R&D organizations.

Semiconductor Research Corporation

SRC was formed in 1982 as a nonprofit institution to fund university research in silicon-based semiconductor research. Its purposes are to advance the technology and to build the base of graduate students trained in semiconductor design and manufacture. The SRC initiative came from the board of the Semiconductor Industry Association (SIA). As Gordon Moore, then a vice president of Intel, recalled on the occasion of SRC's tenth anniversary in 1992:

> The idea was that by pooling the support they were giving to university research, the companies in the [semiconductor manufacturing] industry could have a real impact on the direction that university research took. So the members of the SIA got together and formed SRC, the idea being it would make research more efficient and that it would supply some direction that would have the effect of dragging some of the other research money along with it by orienting professors at various universities in the direction of problems that were of interest to us. Even when they were looking for government funding, their interests would be influenced by what the industry was doing.[15]

As of 1995, SRC's total annual funding amounted to $36 million for contract research, of which a third came from SEMATECH. There are sixty-one members in three categories: members, affiliate members, and associate members.[16] Except for DOD's Advanced Research Project Agency (ARPA), all of SEMATECH's participants were also members of SRC. To qualify for SRC membership, a company must be substantially owned and controlled by U.S. or Canadian citizens.

With thirty-eight employees in total, including nine technical personnel, SRC operates with a simplified organizational structure designed basically for research planning, R&D contract placement and monitoring, and technology transfer through publications and mentoring programs. Administrative costs amount to 13 percent of its total budget. Its board of directors includes representatives of the ten member companies that pay

TABLE 1.3 Selected Data on Six U.S. R&D Consortia, 1995

	SEMATECH	Semiconductor Research Corporation	Microelectronics and Computer Technology Corporation
Year Founded	1988	1982	1982
Membership			
Number of Firms	10	61	46
Constituencies	Major semiconductor manufacturers and OEM (original equipment manufacturers) purchasers	Semiconductor and electronics firms	Firms in the semiconductor, computer, defense, aerospace, telecommunications, software, and chemicals industries; government and university affiliates
Restrictions	U.S. firms only	U.S. and Canadian firms only	U.S. and Canadian firms only
Number of Employees	800	38	150
1995 Revenues	$180 million	$36 million	$25 million
Mission	Solve the technical challenges required to keep the U.S. number one in the global semiconductor industry. Primary focus: semiconductor manufacturing equipment and materials infrastructure development.	Solve the technical challenges required to keep the U.S. number one in the global semiconductor industry. Primary focus: semiconductor design and manufacturing technology research.	Provide consortial research and development services, mapping precompetitive technology in advanced electronics and information technology, to the requirements for seamless global business operations.

TABLE 1.3 Selected Data on Six U.S. R&D Consortia, 1995 (continued)

	Electric Power Research Institute	Gas Research Institute	Bell Communications Research
Year Founded	1973	1978	1983
Membership			
Number of Firms	700+	310	7
Constituencies	Electricity industry	Gas producers, inter- and intrastate pipelines, and local gas distributors	Telecommunications firms
Restrictions	None	None	Limited to the seven regional Bell operating companies
Number of Employees	600+	250	6,172
1995 Revenues	Approximately $500 million	$190 million	$1.08 billion
Mission	Discover, develop, and deliver high-value technological advances through networking and partnership with the electricity industry.	Discover, develop, and deploy new technologies and information that measurably benefit gas customers and the industry. To enhance the value of gas energy service through planning and managing a consumer-sensitive, cooperative research program emphasizing technology transfer.	Be the worldwide information industry's first choice for innovative and comprehensive networking solutions.

the largest annual dues, as well as six others selected from the remaining members, plus the SRC's president and CEO.

SRC's research program is carried out through annually renewable contracts, with defined progress points and contract reviews conducted by SRC's technical personnel and member-company representatives. The approval of a research project by SRC's research management committee is contingent upon having a member-company mentor in place, to provide assistance—not critiques or redirection—to the faculty-student research team. Assistance might come, for example, in the form of relevant technical information, or the use of a test facility and other services. Mentors are expected to keep in close touch with the researchers through four to six on-site meetings a year. In 1995, 252 faculty members at fifty universities, 813 students, and 453 SRC member-company representatives were involved in mentoring relationships.

Microelectronics and Computer Technology Corporation[17]

MCC was founded in 1982 as a for-profit Delaware corporation to "conduct high-risk, long-range research aimed at significant advances in microelectronics and computer technology." Over the next decade, however, MCC's mission evolved into "enhancing the competitiveness of our members through collaborative research, development, and the deployment of information technologies."

MCC's founding shareholders—twelve in number—represented three major U.S. industries. One group included computer manufacturers: Sperry, NCR, CDC, Honeywell, and DEC. A second group included five semiconductor manufacturers—AMD, Motorola, National Semiconductor, Harris, and Mostek—all of which had suffered from Japan's ascent to world leadership in the DRAM (dynamic random access memory) market. The large aerospace manufacturers—Boeing, Rockwell International, Martin Marietta, and Lockheed—constituted a third shareholder group, each greatly dependent on defense contracting. Finally, as conglomerates, General Electric, 3M, Westinghouse, and AlliedSignal had interests in two or all three of those industries. As of early 1995, MCC had forty-six members.[18] They represented such diverse industries and sectors as microelectronics, electronics, defense, aerospace, computers, telecommunications, software, chemicals, government, and higher education. Total membership had declined from over 80 in 1994.

Total contributions from MCC members grew from $45 million in 1985 to $73 million by 1987, then decreased to $63 million in 1989, $40 million in 1993, and $38 million in 1994. Of the last amount, 42 percent came from member companies, 48 percent from government agencies, and 10 percent from royalties, commercial contracts, and other sources. The price of a share of stock, pegged originally at $150,000, rose to $1 million in 1985 and 1986, after which it dropped to $250,000.

The primary benefit of MCC membership is the opportunity to participate in selected MCC research projects, for specified fees based on project costs. The resulting intellectual property rights are held by MCC.[19] Other benefits include workshops, seminars, and conferences conducted by MCC project managers; an E-mail system offering information on R&D developments, MCC technical abstracts, and Japanese and European technical literature; reports and forecasts prepared by a staff of ten scientists and analysts in MCC's international liaison office; and MCC's partnering-opportunity information service, a database of collaborative and business opportunities in and among member companies.

Soon after it was founded, MCC developed a cafeteria-style research agenda, allowing members to choose from a menu of projects those in which they had an interest and were willing to support. Annual membership dues do not fund a common agenda, as they do in other R&D consortia. As of 1994, 85 percent of the technical staff were full-time MCC employees, compared with 40 percent of SEMATECH's technical staff.

Electric Power Research Institute

The oldest of the six consortia, EPRI was founded in 1973. In 1995, of the approximately three thousand electric utilities in the United States, more than 700 were members of EPRI. Though they represented less than 25 percent of all electric utilities, they accounted for 70 percent of the total retail kilowatt-hours (kwh) of electricity produced in this country.[20] Total EPRI revenues in that year amounted to over $500 million. Each member contributed in direct proportion to the number of retail kilowatt-hours it produced.

EPRI's RD&D (research, development, and demonstration) program has these broad purposes: to build the utility power load by developing products for which electricity would be the preferred energy source (e.g., heat pumps for residential and commercial heating and cooling); to improve the quality and cost efficiency of electric power generation, transmission, and distribution (e.g., electronic power controls, to reduce operating costs); to address environmental and safety issues posed by the utilities themselves (e.g., NO_x emissions control) or soluble by them (e.g., biomedical waste treatment); and to develop cost-efficient alternatives for power generation beyond the use of existing coal- and oil-based technologies (e.g., solar power, wind power).

EPRI's R&D programs are carried out through agreements with external contractors. In most cases, they are companies that have the capability for product and service development, as well as follow-up commercialization or market development. Target products include new technology for member-company use in power generation, transmission, and distribution; technology for industrial electric power applications; and consumer end products that use electricity. As of 1995, a technical staff of almost three hundred administered more than three thousand R&D agreements covering more than two thousand active projects.

Gas Research Institute

In 1973, the same year EPRI began operating, leaders in the natural gas industry took initiatives that led ultimately to the formation of the Gas Research Institute, which was modeled after EPRI. Articles of incorporation for the institute were filed in July 1976, and application for funding was made to the Federal Power Commission in 1977. GRI began operating in 1978. According to the articles of incorporation:

> The corporation is organized exclusively for scientific and educational purposes . . . to conduct programs of applied and basic research . . . in order to assist all segments of the gas industry in meeting the critical demands for energy and raw materials of the United States by providing adequate, reliable, and safe, economical and environmentally acceptable gas service to the benefit of the public.

GRI's membership includes gas suppliers, both the major gas and oil producers and the smaller independents; transporters, both interstate and intrastate pipelines; distributors, both investor-owned (private) utilities and community-owned municipals; and industrial consumers. Thus, the consortium is vertically organized. GRI's R&D program runs the gamut, from developing new technologies for exploration and production to producing natural gas substitutes and developing more efficient gas distribution and end-use systems for both industrial and consumer applications. Like EPRI, GRI carries out its R&D program through contractual arrangements with commercializing partners, most of them suppliers of industrial and consumer products used in the production, transmission, and consumption of natural gas.

As of 1995, GRI had 310 members plus 23 nonvoting associate members, most of whom were foreign gas companies. It operated on a budget of approximately $200 million, most of which was funded through a surcharge levied on GRI's interstate pipeline members, based on their natural gas throughput.

Bell Communications Research

Bellcore was established in 1983, pursuant to a consent decree ordering the divestiture by AT&T of those portions of its business that provided local telecommunications and exchange access. The decree, approved by Judge Harold J. Greene, United States District Judge for the District of Columbia, permitted the twenty-two divested companies, later grouped into seven independent regional operating companies, to support and share the costs of an organization to perform engineering, administrative, and other services most efficiently provided on a centralized basis.[21] It also required the divested companies to provide a point of contact for coordinating national security and emergency preparedness.

The largest of the R&D consortia in the United States, Bellcore employed 6,172 people in 1995. Owned by the seven regional Bell operating companies, its total revenues amounted in 1995 to $1.08 billion: $834 million from its client-owners and $246 million from products and services supplied to nonowner clients, including Cincinnati Bell, the Southern New England Telephone Company, and local telephone companies in the United States and Canada.

Like MCC, Bellcore relies primarily on its internal technology staff of more than four thousand recruited initially from AT&T, Bell Labs, and Western Electric. Currently, a significant portion of its work is carried out jointly with technical personnel in the seven regional Bell organizations. It also has extensive partnering arrangements with a wide range of domestic and foreign companies.

SOME OBSERVATIONS AND COMPARISONS

The six consortia discussed here have much in common, though they differ in regard to membership composition, funding levels and sources, government involvement, R&D sourcing patterns, and mission. All were formed to meet urgent needs at the industry and national levels. EPRI and GRI were started in response to watershed events, such as the power blackout of 1965 in the northeastern United States and Canada, the Arab oil embargo of 1973, and the natural gas shortages of the early 1970s—all of which raised a national alarm over the reliability of the nation's power supplies. Other contributing factors were the emergence of environmental issues as an urgent public concern, and the recognition of government and industry leaders that the electric power and natural gas industries lacked an adequate technology base to meet the expanding national demand for power.

MCC and SEMATECH were formed in response to Japan's rising dominance of world markets for semiconductors, semiconductor manufacturing equipment, and the end products in which integrated circuits are an integral component. SRC answered the need of major semiconductor manufacturers and consumers for academic research in semiconductor design and manufacture.

Within the group, comparing MCC with SEMATECH, on the one hand, and EPRI with GRI, on the other, may be useful. In each pair, the two consortia were borne out of common concerns, to carry out comparable missions. SEMATECH and MCC responded to the Japanese threat in the global markets for semiconductors and microelectronics. GRI and EPRI were formed to meet a national need to assure the domestic energy supply and satisfy rapidly growing consumption. Yet SEMATECH and MCC evolved in dramatically different directions, as did GRI and EPRI.

A nonprofit organization, SEMATECH has focused on infrastructure development in the semiconductor industry, relying largely on suppliers of manufacturing equipment as an external research resource. From its inception, SEMATECH has been supported by government funding to the extent of half its total R&D budget of approximately $200 million a year. SEMATECH's membership is small and quite cohesive. The consortium is widely credited with having reestablished a viable base for semiconductor equipment manufacturing in the United States and with leading the rapid advance of semiconductor manufacturing technology.

By comparison, MCC is a for-profit corporation that depends largely on its internal staff of technologists to carry out its R&D program under contract to small groups of member companies and government agencies. Compared with SEMATECH, MCC has a much larger, more disparate membership—more than eighty members in 1994—and a much smaller budget. Though it was created to take on the Japanese in the advance of microelectronics technology, that mission has faded in favor of enhancing the competitiveness of member companies.

Compared with SEMATECH and MCC, EPRI and GRI are much less constrained by competitive rivalry among member companies. They therefore serve a broad range of R&D needs in areas such as operations technology, supply industry infrastructure development, market development for new end products, personnel training, and environmental health and safety engineering. In so doing, EPRI and GRI account for a much larger percentage—often more than half—of their member companies' R&D budgets, compared with SEMATECH and MCC.

Though both EPRI and GRI serve regulated energy industries and pursue broad industry development goals, they too have evolved quite differently. Given the Federal Energy Regulatory Commission's jurisdiction over interstate pipelines, GRI is tightly regulated with regard to funding level, program and project approval, and annual reporting procedure. GRI has also been the target of interest groups seeking to cap its R&D budget and limit the scope of its work. Furthermore, GRI is vertically structured. Its membership and governance bodies represent gas exploration and production companies, interstate and intrastate gas pipelines, local distribution companies, state regulatory commissions, and large industrial consumers. Yet the great bulk of GRI's funding comes just from one of these constituents, interstate pipelines. GRI's annual revenues are only about one-third those of EPRI.

By comparison, EPRI is horizontally structured; its members are all electric power producers, each of which contributes to the consortium's funding in an amount proportional to its retail kilowatt-hour output. While the fifty state utility commissions pass on the admissibility of membership dues in calculating the rates utilities may charge consumers, EPRI's programs and budget levels are not subject to the scrutiny and approval of federal agencies. One factor that might explain the substantial difference in the size and scope of operations in the two consortia is EPRI's greater freedom from regulatory intervention.

The chapter that follows develops the thesis that the three essential elements of a successful consortium are a compelling initial vision, a sustainable mission, and strong leadership. Then, moving into issues central to consortium management, chapter 3 explores the R&D planning process, in particular the influences that may come to bear in setting the R&D agenda. Chapter 4 looks at the five key elements of consortium strategy: membership delineation, funding mechanisms and formulas, R&D sourcing arrangements, the R&D product lines and technology delivery systems. The delivery of technology is further elaborated in chapter 5, "Technology Transfer as Marketing." Chapter 6 moves the discussion to a macro level, providing an overview of R&D consortia in the United States, Japan, and Europe—the conditions that have led to the rise of R&D consortia over the last quarter century, as well as current trends in collaborative enterprise in each area and their relative success. Chapter 7 reviews the existing body of theory on collective action and suggests ways in which it may be extended, based on the United States' experience with R&D consortia. Chapter 8 then considers the role consortia play in the U.S. economy and their effect on industrial development and competition. It also reviews lessons gleaned from managerial experience regarding the critical success factors in forming and managing collaborative R&D ventures.

CHAPTER 2

Consortium Formation:
Vision, Mission, and Leadership

The six consortia described in chapter 1 were born out of a sense of industry crisis and/or a deeply sensed need to advance the cause of industry R&D. In each instance, industry and/or government leaders articulated the need, advocated collective endeavor, and called for action. The vision was then translated into a mission, reworked often by the founding leaders, government bodies, and industry associations—and in Bellcore's case, by the courts. A compelling vision, a viable mission, and strong leadership— these are the foundations of a successful consortium.

Vision is the basis for a call to action. The validity of a vision may depend on the stature of those sounding the call, and on the premise that certain objectives can be met more effectively in a collective endeavor rather than as an undertaking of a single firm.

If vision is the basis of collective action, mission is an articulation of purpose. To be sustainable, a mission must promise the fulfillment of some broadly perceived need at the industry or sector level. It should attract the support of relevant constituencies—those whose backing can contribute to the consortium's success, or whose lack of support could jeopardize its success from the outset. Depending on the mission and the consortium's anticipated membership group, relevant constituencies might include industry or sector market leaders and trade associations. If a consortium has a national purpose, it may be essential to have the positive intervention of concerned government bodies, as well.

Along with a clear and achievable mission, the importance of effective leadership cannot be overstated, both at the outset and in successive management generations. In the formative stages of a consortium, the leader typically exerts a critical, if not defining, influence on mission, formulation, consortium policies, governance structures and processes, and strategy. He or she makes a significant initial contribution in gaining the support of the industry sector the consortium has been formed to serve, attracting membership and funding and forming relationships with external constituencies such as government bodies, trade associations, and public interest groups. Equally important is the leader's ability to attract human resources—in particular, skilled technical and administrative personnel.

This chapter draws on the experiences of the Electric Power Research Institute, Microelectronics and Computer Technology Corporation, and Bellcore to stress the influence of vision, mission, and leadership on the viability and success of a consortium.

THE ELECTRIC POWER RESEARCH INSTITUTE

The vision for EPRI came from Joseph C. Swidler, who was at the time chairman of the Federal Power Commission. In a speech given in 1963, at a meeting of the Edison Electric Institute (EEI), Swidler urged the formation of an industry-wide research program. His speech concluded with these comments:

> I am convinced, and many industry leaders to whom I have talked share the conviction, that the scale of research in the electric power field is too small and that the allocation of research effort is too haphazard. The electric power industry is too great and important, and its potentials are far too vast for its research strength to depend either upon the initiative and the particular interests of individual electric industry executives who are harried with operating responsibilities, or upon the "fallout" from research programs directed at altogether different objectives. The Nation's No. 1 industry can afford a research program scaled to its needs and opportunities. It cannot afford the risk of lost opportunities and delayed progress which is inherent in the present lack of system or direction in research.
>
> I have no prescription for curing the research problem of the industry but I should like to propose a small step which could lead to some improvement. As the agency with overall national responsibility in the power supply field, the FPC could appropriately call together a group of knowledgeable people representing the private, public and cooperative sectors of the industry, the manufacturers, and the research community, to consider how the industry—acting as a whole—could best serve its own interests and the interests of the nation by stimulating more intensive research efforts. . . .
>
> The FPC seeks no role in such an organization. Our only interest is that the industry itself—all of the elements of the industry—shall create and maintain an organization which will assure the utmost technological advancement which can

CONSORTIUM FORMATION **3 1**

be brought about by research and development activities on a scale commensurate with the opportunities and promise of rewards. Here, indeed, is a goal on which all of the forces of the industry can unite to advance.[1]

In 1971 Senators Warren Magnuson and Ernest Hollings, respectively chairman of the Senate Commerce Committee and one of its ranking majority members, introduced legislation (S.R. 1684) to create a federal fund to support research and development for the electric utility industry. Its work was to be funded by a tax of 0.15 mills per kwh, or about $300 million annually at current levels of power generation.[2] Industry reactions ranged from alarm over the possibility of government control to recognition that some form of collaborative research was greatly needed in the industry.

Spurred by the Magnuson-Hollings initiative, members of the Edison Electric Institute, under the leadership of EEI's chairman, Shearon Harris, turned to a study outlining the industry's R&D needs. It was completed in June 1971 by the Electric Research Council, a group organized in 1965 by investor-owned and public utilities to consider the needs of the electric industry. The report proposed a $3 billion research program that the industry itself, rather than the government, might undertake over the next three decades.

The National Association of Regulated Utility Commissioners (NARUC) strongly endorsed the EEI program. George Bloom, chairman of NARUC's committee on energy research and development, testified before the Senate that "sharply increased research and development in the energy field is mandatory if the nation is to accomplish the twin goals of adequate and economical power for consumers, and preserving our environmental heritage for ourselves and the generations yet to come."[3] Although they were skeptical, Senators Magnuson and Hollings agreed to give Harris and the EEI a year to develop support and funding for an industry-managed R&D program. The proposed consortium, the Electric Power Research Institute (EPRI), began operations in 1973.

From the outset, EPRI's mission covered the broad range of the electric utility industry's R&D needs in areas such as power generation and delivery, end-use product and technology development, and environmental sensitivity. In setting the R&D agenda, there were no concerns about trespassing on what member companies might regard as proprietary technology, essential to their competitive advantage. The industry operated essentially as a regulated monopoly, with each participant occupying its own geographic area. This condition contrasted sharply with that of the semiconductor industry, where consortia members were locked in competitive rivalry, and R&D consortia agendas had to be planned to avoid members' proprietary research interests.

EPRI's mission attracted a membership that was relatively homogeneous, consisting as it did of investor-owned and federal utilities (the Tennessee Valley Authority and the Bonneville Power Administration), co-ops, and municipal utilities—all in the business of generating and delivering electric power.

In 1972 Dr. Chauncey Starr was selected to be EPRI's first president and chief executive officer. At age 60, Starr was dean of UCLA's School of Applied Engineering. Shearon Harris had met Starr at a seminar at Georgia Tech. He spoke with him about the concept of an industry-managed R&D center. As Starr remembered:

> I thought a lot about it and then I wrote him a six-page letter which covered (1) the role of electricity in societal development and the responsibility of the utility industry, (2) the opportunity to make electricity a force for real change in society, and (3) the stodginess of the industry in meeting these needs. The industry, I said in my letter, was stuck-in-the-mud, mundane, and short-sighted.[4]

Before World War II, Starr had been a research associate at MIT and had expected to pursue an academic career. But the Navy's Bureau of Ships called him to organize a research group on counter devices for underwater mines. Two years later he was called to the Manhattan Project and sent to the Oak Ridge National Laboratory to manage a laboratory of more than two thousand engineers, all military personnel.

Following the war, Starr joined North American Aviation (NAA) to work on an Air Force project involving the application of nuclear power to rockets. The assignment completed, he became head of a three-thousand-person NAA unit assigned to develop nuclear power-generation technology for the Atomic Energy Commission. He remained at NAA, which was subsequently acquired by Rockwell International, until 1966, when he returned to academic life as dean of engineering at UCLA.

In mid-December 1972 Starr was called by Harris to head the newly proposed Electric Power Research Institute. As Starr recalled,

> I agreed to take the job but on my terms: it would be a five-year contract; the industry could look over my shoulder and make suggestions, but they could not interfere with the management. Those were the terms; I had a five-year shot and, to start with, $60 million in pledged funds.[5]

By this time the Institute had been registered as a nonprofit corporation to conduct a national R&D program for the production, transmission, distribution, and use of electric energy. With the Magnuson bill still pending, Harris and other members of the search committee were under pressure to launch EPRI as soon as possible.

Starr's experience as a large-scale research manager and his personal values shaped the policies he established at EPRI in the early years—policies that endured. First, EPRI would involve its members in developing goals, determining research priorities, and reviewing research programs. Industry representatives at all levels of the organization would review, advise, and comment, but would have no decision-making authority.[6]

Second, EPRI would use outside contractors rather than build an in-house research staff. According to Starr,

> What the selection committee had in mind was something like Bell Labs. But I'd been in R&D all my life, and I know the amount of time and dollars it takes to build and staff a physical facility. I figured it would take ten years and a billion dollars, and we'd have to steal talent from other R&D labs. The industry wouldn't be that patient.
>
> Subcontracting research, rather than building an in-house capability, turned out to be a good choice for other reasons. It enabled us to be more flexible in our R&D programs, as member interests and research needs have changed over the past decade.[7]

It is interesting to note that relying on external R&D sources was inconsistent with Swidler's vision and with the recommendations of the Electric Research Council's task force, an industry group convened by Swidler and Harris. The task force report had specifically stated, "EPRI should undertake to acquire an independent research capability rather than confine its efforts to the funding of research by others."[8]

Third, Starr decided early on that societal interests would be an important factor in shaping EPRI's agenda. He would have an advisory council comprised of selected regulatory commissioners and other nonmember leaders, who out of experience and breadth of perspective would function as a window on social needs and national research priorities.

Still another of Starr's policy decisions was that EPRI would not serve as an advocate for industry positions. As Starr noted:

> In the first few years, we had a little trouble with that one among our utility members, but it was important to establish our integrity. Now an EPRI technical report is regarded as a solid technical statement. We provide the industry with a technology base for the policy positions *they* want to take. EPRI's integrity means a great deal to us *and* to the industry.[9]

Finally, EPRI would willingly cofund research programs with government agencies, but would not act as a research contractor for the government. Working under government contract at NAA, Starr had found that project approvals were slow and that government auditing and reporting requirements were burdensome.

Starr served as EPRI's president for five years, continuing as vice chairman of the board of directors. He was succeeded in late 1978 by Floyd Culler, a veteran of thirty years at the Oak Ridge National Laboratory, where he had risen to the positions of deputy and acting director. Culler had received numerous awards in recognition of his work in nuclear energy, especially for his contributions to chemical processing, radioactive waste management, and reactor research and development. He had also served on nuclear-power-related advisory committees in a number of universities and government agencies.

Early in his tenure as EPRI's president, Culler recognized an urgent need to go beyond R&D and find better ways to deliver new technology to member utilities. Among other initiatives, Culler oversaw the development of demonstration centers across the country as showcases for new technical advances. He also redefined EPRI's mission as RD&D (research, development, and demonstration).

In 1988 Richard Balzhiser became president of EPRI. He had joined the consortium in 1973, as the first technical division manager, and had risen to the position of executive vice president in 1987. With a doctorate in chemical engineering, Balzhiser had had a distinguished career both in government and academia. When Starr recruited him to join the newly formed consortium, he was serving as assistant director in the Office of Science and Technology, where he directed energy, environment, and natural resources programs. Before that he had been chairman of the department of chemical engineering at the University of Michigan. Throughout his career, Balzhiser had served on numerous scientific and technical advisory boards.

The governance structure that Starr put in place, again, reflected his own concepts of EPRI's role in the American economy. Thus, the model Starr established early on at EPRI, and adopted later by the Gas Research Institute, shows how structure and process respond to the interests of a large membership and multiple constituencies. At EPRI the top governance bodies are the board of directors, on which each membership constituency holds a number of seats, and the advisory council, which represents public interest groups, the scientific and academic communities, and concerned state and federal agencies.

The twenty-four-member board of directors is composed of chief executive officers of electric utilities. Sixteen come from investor-owned utilities, three from municipal utilities, three from cooperatives, and one each from the Tennessee Valley Authority and the Bonneville Power Administration. Each year's slate of candidates for the board originates from the recommendations of existing board members, industry trade associations, and EPRI's management, though the nominations for all but the TVA and BPA are actually made by the trade associations.

The thirty-member advisory council includes EPRI's CEO and former EPRI presidents Starr and Culler, ex-officio members. In addition to the ten members representing NARUC, the council includes representatives of public interest groups, such as The Nature Conservancy and Resources for the Future; of university faculties; and of government agencies—for example, the Natural Resources Defense Council and the Office of Technology Assessment. Although it has no voting power, the advisory council serves as a link with the scientific community, reflects societal interests, and coordinates the consortium's R&D programs with related work going on in university and government laboratories. Thus it helps to establish the consortium's R&D priorities. At both EPRI and GRI, the advisory council's input feeds into the research planning process at the board level and below. In addition, advisory council members link the consortium with the constituencies they represent, lending legitimacy to the consortium's mission in the eyes of its external constituencies.

The advisory council plays a particular role in EPRI and GRI governance, for two reasons. Each consortium serves a regulated industry in which problems of environmental health and safety and the costs of energy to consumers are matters of public interest. Furthermore, each has an R&D program, the planning of which is influenced by national priorities, and must often be coordinated with comparable initiatives in government-funded programs and university research centers.

By 1995, EPRI was playing a key role in the advancement of technology for the generation and distribution of electric power. Its more than seven hundred members rely on EPRI as their major R&D resource. Through its R&D program, the consortium has contributed to the development of both the industry supply infrastructure and its end-product markets. The net benefits, both measurable and unmeasurable, have been considerable. For example, EPRI members estimate that they may be realizing a more than threefold return on their membership dues. At New England Electric Systems (NEES), a study spanning a recent three-year period identified 252 EPRI technology products, of which 220 were classified as beneficial. More than 60 percent of those products have been put to use. The benefits were quantifiable, however, for only 27 products (12 percent of the total). On those products alone, the returns to NEES were calculated at $11.9 million, or 3.5 times the cost to the utility of its EPRI membership over the three-year period. Overall, EPRI managers estimated that by 1993, the Institute had returned $36 billion in benefits to its members, their industrial customers, and society at large over the twenty years of its existence.

The foundations of EPRI's record of accomplishment were Joseph Swidler's vision, a clear mission, and an R&D program that added demonstrable value to the electric power industry in general and its members in particular. EPRI had wide support from industry, governmental, and other constituencies. Its governance structure reflects both the need to involve a large and diverse membership and to provide for inputs from EPRI's many external constituencies. EPRI's success can by attributed as well to its leadership, in particular founding CEO Chauncey Starr. As it turned out, Starr was probably right in opting for outside R&D sourcing, because much of EPRI's work is focused on supply-industry infrastructure and end-product market development—domains in which it is important to involve firms operating at these levels in the R&D program. Starr's successors, Floyd Culler and Richard Balzhiser, also contributed to EPRI's development, particularly in establishing the consortium's R&D delivery capabilities (see chapter 5, "Technology Transfer as Marketing").

In sum, EPRI's mission as defined by Starr did not depart significantly from Joseph Swidler's vision, endorsed by the Edison Electric Institute, the National Association of Regulated Utility Commissioners, and in its broad purpose, by Senators Magnuson and Hollings. However, Starr gave it form with regard to its policies, governance structure, R&D sourcing strategy, and relations with external constituencies. Clearly, in these respects EPRI reflects his values and the lessons of his experience. The fact that EPRI has survived for more than two decades and grown in scope and achievement is testimony to the enduring nature of Starr's influence and the contributions of his successors.

MICROELECTRONICS AND COMPUTER TECHNOLOGY CORPORATION

MCC[10] was the vision of William C. Norris, CEO of Control Data. He believed that a consortium of U.S. semiconductor and computer manufacturers would be an essential vehicle for sharing the heavy research costs of rapidly advancing technology and meeting Japanese competition head on. Norris first proposed his ideas in spring 1981, but he met with skepticism. Reflecting prevailing sentiments, H. Glenn Haney, vice president for strategic planning and development at Sperry Univac, was quoted as saying, "The very essence of our business technology is the chips and electronics. To willingly put the core of your R&D thrust outside your own control and share it with competitors is basically unattractive."[11]

It was not until the industry had "had the hell scared out of them," according to Norris, by a speech given at a trade association conference in April 1981 by Control Data's president, Bob Price, that computer company leaders were moved to action. Price predicted that within the decade the only important global computer companies would be Japan, Inc., IBM, and perhaps AT&T. In February 1982 Norris convened a meeting in Orlando of fifty senior-level executives from seventeen leading computer builders and semiconductor manufacturers. At that meeting, his vision became a reality.

Retired Admiral Bobby Ray Inman was the board of directors' top choice to head the newly established consortium. A native Texan, Inman had graduated from the University of Texas in 1950 and entered the Naval Reserve in 1951; he had served in both the Korean and Vietnam wars. From 1972 to 1977 Inman had directed Naval Intelligence, before becoming director of the National Security Agency. With his promotion to the rank of admiral in 1981, Inman was assigned to the post of deputy director of the Central Intelligence Agency. After he retired from government service in 1982, with the permanent rank of admiral, he had become involved in a broad range of community, public service, and business activities.

Inman had a reputation for honesty and integrity. He was also known by top managers in several of MCC's founding companies, having been directly involved in the purchase of large computers for government use. A luncheon speech he had given in San Francisco about a year before MCC was formed, on the United States' loss of leadership in the global electronics industry and the threat it posed to the nation's security, had attracted considerable media attention.

According to Gibson and Rogers in *R&D Collaboration on Trial,* Inman brought several important qualities to MCC: a national identity, important in attracting media attention and public recognition; an insider's knowledge of Washington; a reputation for unquestioned integrity; and an "intelligence" point of view.[12]

Attracting qualified researchers to MCC was an early challenge for Inman. Ultimately, he sought and received authorization from the board of directors to recruit scientists from the outside, for both administrative and technical positions.[13] As Inman explained, "I did not want to preside over a turkey farm. . . . The reality was that the talent was not in the companies or they didn't make it available, and I think it was the former."[14] Since research talent was not forthcoming from member companies, Inman set out to attract scientists from prestigious universities, federal laboratories, and nonmember corporate laboratories. Doing so allowed MCC to reach full staffing more quickly.

MCC had been conceived to counter the threat posed by the announcement in 1981 of the Japanese Fifth Generation Computer Project, also known as ICOT. ICOT's purpose was to develop a machine with artificial intelligence capability—a system that could learn, draw inferences, and make decisions. The project had been funded at $1.35 billion for ten years, with a third of that amount coming from the Japanese government. ICOT had followed on the heels of the very successful VLSI project (1976 to 1979) to develop the technology for large-scale integrated circuits. That effort had culminated with the announcement in 1980 of a prototype 256K RAM chip. VLSI consortium members included Japan's largest electronics companies: NEC, Toshiba, Hitachi, Mitsubishi Electric, and Fujitsu. These firms had had 15 percent of the merchant DRAM market in 1976; by 1981, they had 70 percent.

Following ICOT's example, MCC's mission was "to conduct high-risk long-range research aimed at significant advances in microelectronics and computer technology." Specifically, it was to:

- preserve and enhance U.S. predominance and preeminence in microelectronics and computing;
- cooperate at the base technology level, to provide long-term benefit to the industry and the nation;
- recognize the immediate threat in microelectronics and the long-term threat in computing;
- avoid the anticompetitive effects of the eventual concentration of both industries in a few very large, vertically integrated entities.

The mission failed, however, to attract the kind of government support extended later to SEMATECH; and more important, it did not attract IBM, the computer industry's market leader. (In fact, the last item on the list above would seem to cast IBM in the role of an MCC competitor.)

According to Dr. John Armstrong, IBM's chief scientist from 1986 to 1989, "IBM did not join MCC and never took it seriously. What MCC was attempting to do could better be done by IBM itself and have more potential for competitive advantage if done alone. Also, MCC had too many programs and too little funding, less than $20 million."[15]

According to Dr. Craig Fields, who became MCC's third president in February 1991, as the threat from ICOT receded, it became increasingly difficult to sustain cooperation on long-term research. By late 1991 Fields had formulated his own ideas of MCC's mission for the coming decade: "First of all, absolutely, unambiguously, we're here to give competitive benefits to our 52 member companies [shareholders and associates] . . . and if we end up with substantial federal funding we will have to add the public interest."[16] Thus, as of 1992, the consortium's stated purpose was "to strengthen and sustain the competitiveness of member companies who share common elements of a vision in information technology."

Interviewed in 1993, Dr. Fields elaborated on his concept of MCC's goals: (1) to build business for MCC's member companies, (2) to benefit the United States, (3) to advance science and technology that is of interest to both member companies and MCC's staff, (4) to provide stable careers for MCC personnel so that the first three purposes may be accomplished, and (5) to make it possible for MCC's key contributors to build their personal wealth.[17]

Thus by 1993, MCC's purposes addressed the needs and interests of three constituencies—member companies, the nation, and MCC personnel. Dr. Fields commented further: "Among these goals, there may be some conflict, and tradeoffs may be needed for MCC to work in the balanced best interests of its several constituencies."[18]

While MCC's mission evolved and became more complex with changes in the competitive environment of the semiconductor and computer industries, the fact that it had been incorporated in the state of Delaware as a private profit-making venture was also clouding its mission. The reason for establishing the consortium as a Delaware corporation, as Fields understood it, had been to avoid the public disclosure requirements imposed on nonprofit organizations. Was MCC in business to make a profit, or was it not? According to Fields, "I want to make a profit but not too much because it comes out of our members' pockets."[19]

Dr. Grant Dove, MCC's chairman of the board, saw the consortium's for-profit status as a discipline:

It brings us closer to a private enterprise mentality. With a profit orientation, you have to sell constantly and you have to be focused on creating value. You have to be able to do the job for what you said it would cost. So the purpose is not to make a profit but to influence the way we look at what we do. And anything we make goes to lowering the cost of research.[20]

Consistent with the profit motive was the emergence of another facet of MCC's mission strategy, the launching of entrepreneurial spinoffs. Under Grant Dove, MCC's second CEO, several MCC scientists, frustrated by the failure of member companies to commercialize their new technologies and encouraged by Dove, sought permission to start spinoff ventures to take the technologies to market. But with one exception, their petitions were denied by MCC's board of directors. Shareholders, it seemed, were concerned that others would gain the benefit of work they had funded, and wanted to preserve the option of commercializing the new technologies on their own timetables.

Although spinoff ventures were discouraged in the late 1980s, they were strongly fostered early in Dr. Fields' tenure as CEO. Fields saw them as a viable approach if spinoff ventures could serve as suppliers to MCC member companies, and/or if they could become a source of equity appreciation and investment return for MCC and for their funders. Four such ventures were launched from 1991 to 1993. Commenting on this development, Fields said:

I'm happy because it makes it easier to recruit and I have an equity base to increase my cash flow and a royalty stream. That means more financial stability for MCC. The staff is happy because it gives them career paths and entrepreneurial potential. The investors are happy because they have a lower investment risk. The members are happy because they are building up a base of suppliers to give them preferential access to new technology. Other relationships are also possible. For example, a large member company is now marketing the product of a small spinoff company world wide.[21]

In sum, MCC's vision was born of the sense of crisis created by the announcement of ICOT. When ICOT's threat diminished, MCC's mission to conduct high-risk long-range research became difficult to sustain, and increasingly, its focus turned to serving members' short-term interests, through a series of projects for which each participant paid an equal share. Furthermore, MCC's status as a for-profit corporation had to create a sense of ambivalence about its mission among member shareholders. Any attempt to maximize profits could only come at a higher cost to member companies for the R&D projects they sponsored.

On March 1, 1994, Dr. Craig Fields submitted his resignation as MCC's CEO. A *Business Week* article noted in part:

> What happened? Fields has spent three-and-a-half stormy years trying to re-make MCC. The research consortium was formed in 1982 by powerful U.S. high-tech companies to counter Japanese initiatives in the computer industry. Despite significant progress in his drive to redirect MCC toward commercial projects and away from blue-sky research, staff morale has plummeted, employees say. Backers such as Hewlett-Packard, Eastman Kodak, Motorola, and others still fund MCC to the tune of $40 million annually, the consortium says, but that's down 27% since Fields started. Of the 20 current members, Boeing and Rockwell are no longer active in the consortium.
>
> For Fields, things came to a head at a four-hour board meeting in Austin on Feb. 28, says an MCC insider. Board members expressed worry about a Fields initiative called MCC Ventures, launched in 1992. Its aim: to speed MCC's innovations to market by backing startups that will use the consortium's technology in commercial development. So far, MCC has launched four spin-offs, in which MCC members have a small financial stake.
>
> But board members were concerned that too much of MCC's resources and management time were being siphoned off by the venture, the insider says. Directors, most of whom have little entrepreneurial experience, also raised questions about the spin-offs' potential for payoffs. Fields pressed for alternatives for getting MCC's technology out of its labs faster. When board members couldn't provide suggestions but remained critical of the venture, both sides agreed Fields should leave.[22]

Following Fields' resignation, the MCC board began a search for a successor, at the same time meeting to review the consortium's mission. The consensus was that MCC would best serve its members in a consortial role, as originally intended—that is, by working in support of members' particular R&D needs. Uncomfortable with spinoffs as an end in itself rather than a vehicle for serving member company needs, the board dissolved MCC Ventures. Among other considerations, the directors were concerned that such entrepreneurial initiatives might result in new competition for member companies. In the future, member companies would choose the mode of making a new technology operational. Possible options were third-party licensing, commercialization by a member company, use within member firms, and partnering with another company. Spinoffs were also an option, if the purpose was to serve MCC members—but not for profit as an end in itself.[23]

The search for a new CEO concluded with the appointment of Dr. John McRary. McRary had previously served as executive vice president of Science Applications International Corporation (SAIC). SAIC, a company with sales of close to $2 billion in 1993, was engaged in developing military systems, computer software, displays, and terminals, factory automation systems, and artificial intelligence/expert systems. According to Grant Dove, "He's to make sure that we don't lose sight of our original mission, and that we don't pursue revenues and profits not in support of the basic mission."[24]

At MCC, a compelling vision turned into an ambivalent mission. Founded in 1982 with ten shareholder members,[25] MCC's total contributions from its members grew from $45 million in 1985 to $73 million in 1987, decreasing to $63 million in 1989 and $38 million in 1994. Almost half the last amount came from government sources. MCC revenues in 1995 amounted to $25 million.

In retrospect, the viability and sustainability of William Norris's vision and MCC's original mission—to "preserve and enhance U.S. predominance and preeminence in microelectronics and computing"—must be questioned. It did not attract the support of relevant government agencies, nor gain IBM's involvement. The scale of funding fell well short of the magnitude of MCC's mission. In a short time, MCC's membership ceased to support the kind of long-term research that had originally been envisioned, particularly as Japan's ICOT threat lost any sense of urgency. After that there was no overarching purpose; successive iterations of MCC's mission seemed only to generate dissension between MCC management and the board, and to cloud MCC's sense of mission.

In the meantime, Inman's early difficulties in attracting qualified member-company personnel at the officer and technical levels played out in the buildup of an internal R&D staff, and in difficulties in transferring new technology to MCC's members.[26] Fields' solution was to turn to spinoffs as a vehicle for dissemination of new technology—a move that alienated key member representatives and led, according to the business media, to his resignation. Though members were apparently not putting new technology to use in a timely manner, they did not want the fruits of their investments to accrue to outside parties.

MCC's original mission statement suggests a unified research program, modeled on VLSI and ICOT, aimed at retaking the U.S. lead in microelectronics and computing. Instead, the consortium evolved into an organization that addressed the R&D needs of those who subscribed to its menu of research programs. Today MCC is confronting a significant decline in both membership and revenues.

BELL COMMUNICATIONS RESEARCH

As noted in chapter 1, Bellcore was formed in 1983, pursuant to a consent decree ordering the divestiture of those portions of AT&T's operating companies that provided local telecommunications and exchange access services. Called the Modified Final Judgment (MFJ), the consent decree was approved with some changes by Judge Harold Greene, U.S. district judge for the District of Columbia. It permitted the twenty-two divested companies, later grouped into the seven regional Bell operating companies (RBOCs), to support and share the costs of certain pooled services: engineering, administrative, and other functions. The consent decree also required the divested companies to provide through Bellcore a point of contact for coordinating national security and emergency preparedness. Both the RBOCs and Bellcore were forbidden to manufacture or provide telecommunications products, except to provide (but not manufacture) customer-premises equipment. Further elaboration by the court in 1987 established that the bar on manufacturing did not apply to the development of software to be used in the design, maintenance, and operation of exchange networks. Nor did the MFJ preclude Bellcore and the operating companies from issuing generic requirements for equipment and testing telecommunications equipment produced by operating company suppliers. In fact, both software development and the technical analysis of equipment became major programs at Bellcore.

Thus, shaped in the context of a court decision, Bellcore would serve essentially as a replacement for Bell Labs—an R&D resource that remained with AT&T—and as a facility for providing the RBOCs with certain pooled services. Bellcore's membership is closed; each of the seven RBOCs owns one share of stock and is represented on the board. No additional shares may be sold without the unanimous consent of the shareholders.

The bar on working directly with the industry equipment supply sector proved frustrating. As one Bellcore manager noted in an interview:

> This has a chilling effect on our efforts. Our people can only go so far and then they have to throw the technology over the wall. If we could go farther, we could work with vendors to the point where the product can be fully brought to commercialization, and we could get better equipment for the owner companies. In addition, we could get some licensing revenue and reduce the risk for the manufacturers.

Bellcore Services

Working within this constraint, Bellcore provided a wide range of services for its seven client-owners:

- definition of new network services;
- definition of new technology and architectures for network evolution;
- development and provision of software for use in operating exchange networks;
- provision of support to RBOC operations;
- issuance of generic requirements for equipment to be purchased by Bell operating companies;
- analysis and testing of telecommunications equipment to be purchased by RBOCs;
- liaison with government agencies and industry standards bodies in the development of industry-wide protocols and standards;
- provision of technical support to RBOCs on regulatory matters;
- development of training programs on industry-specific subjects;
- development and dissemination of information on telecommunications accounting practices and procedures;
- provision of expert testimony at hearings of state regulatory commissions, most often related to the allowance of Bellcore charges as a cost element in RBOC rates.

In addition to providing these services to the seven RBOCs, Bellcore negotiated technology development contracts with other companies in the telecommunications industry. As of 1995, revenue from companies other than the RBOCs amounted to 23 percent of Bellcore's total revenue of $1.08 billion.

As agreed among the shareholders, Bellcore projects fell into two categories: infrastructure and elective projects. The latter were negotiated with Bellcore by individual client-owners or some subset of the consortium membership. Infrastructure projects were supported equally by all shareholders. They were defined as being of potentially substantial benefit to all—technology that, once developed, could not be denied to any shareholder. Each such project was to be approved by five of the seven member firms.

In 1987 the amount of funding for infrastructure projects became the subject of negotiations among the Bellcore operating companies. Objecting strongly to the fact that such projects could be approved by a 5-to-2 vote, US WEST had petitioned to withdraw from the consortium in December

1986. The company wanted, in effect, to have veto power over any proposed infrastructure project of which it did not approve, rather than to pay a share of the project cost. As the price of US WEST's remaining a member company, a 36.7 percent cap was established on infrastructure work (the 5-to-2 approval requirement continued in effect). Increasingly, however, Bellcore's technology resources were applied to elective projects, reducing the infrastructure component to less than the original cap. As of 1995, only 6.25 percent of Bellcore's revenues were allocated to mandatory (infrastructure) projects.

Bellcore's Leadership

Bellcore's first president, Rocco Marano, was an insider. With degrees in business and law from Fordham University, Marano had worked in finance, accounting, and operations since 1953. He had served as comptroller and then operating vice president of New Jersey Bell; operating vice president of New York Telephone; and vice president of staff at AT&T. In 1980 he had been named president of New Jersey Bell, a position he held for two years before becoming Bellcore's first president.

In an interview in 1991, Marano was asked what qualities he believed had made him the choice as Bellcore's CEO. He stated:

> I was the one individual that all seven agreed on. They may have had particular trust in me and my ability to listen. They knew I'd consider each owner's need when I had to make decisions that would affect them all. . . . Patience, that's a quality I knew I had, one that was tested more than once in the earliest days.

Dr. George Heilmeier succeeded Marano in 1991. Heilmeier held a B.S. in electrical engineering from the University of Pennsylvania, and an M.S. and Ph.D. in solid state materials and electronics from Princeton. In 1962, his work in electro-optical effects in liquid crystals at RCA Laboratories led to the first liquid crystal displays in calculators, watches, and instrumentation. In 1970 Heilmeier was appointed assistant director of defense in charge of all DOD research in electronics and the physical sciences. Five years later he became director of DOD's Defense Advanced Research Projects Agency (DARPA), where he launched initiatives in space-based lasers and infra-red technology, stealth aircraft, and artificial intelligence. He left government in 1977 to join Texas Instruments, becoming senior vice president and technical officer in 1983.

Managers at Bellcore and Heilmeier himself thought it significant that Bellcore's directors had gone outside the consortium to find a successor for Marano. In particular, it was thought they had wanted someone from a market-driven business in an unregulated, highly competitive environment in which cost efficiency was critically important. Heilmeier's mandate, developed through negotiation with Bellcore's board, was to:

- develop a ten-year vision for the RBOCs' role in the telecommunications industry;
- provide the RBOCs with revenue-enhancing opportunities;
- provide the RBOCs with opportunities to lower their costs;
- reduce Bellcore's operating costs;
- avoid playing favorites among the seven client-owners.

Asked in an interview early after his appointment why he had accepted the invitation as Marano's successor, Heilmeier said that he strongly believed the telecommunications industry was "where the action is," at least for the next decade. Heilmeier saw Bellcore as a key player in the building of a new information infrastructure, comparable to the historic development of shipping, canals, roads, railroads, and air transportation. Bellcore and the RBOCs, he believed, had the resources to lead such an effort. His concern was that U.S. telecommunications continue to be a strong industry.

Winds of Change

The decade of the 1990s brought tremendous change to the telecommunications industry, which was deregulated at both the state and federal levels, bringing telephone companies into increasingly intense interfirm rivalry. Intraindustry competition was fueled as well by the rise of new entrants. Encouraged by the Federal Communications Commission, cable television companies were developing two-way communications systems with a potential for use as telephone networks. Other new competitors included installers of personal communications networks (PCNs), which enabled callers to bypass the Bell-operated telephone systems. The seven Baby Bells responded by diversifying into a range of other telecommunications-related services and expanding into overseas markets. The seven firms (some more than others) began to build up their own internal R&D resources. As of 1996, the promise of further federally legislated deregulation suggested that the Baby Bells might move aggressively into each other's markets. In fact, some were thought likely to merge with others, a move that would heighten considerably their already intense rivalry.[27]

In October 1994 Bellcore's client-owners surprised observers by announcing they were planning to divest Bellcore. An article in the *New York Times,* "Baby Bells Prepare to Sell Off Bellcore to Resolve Conflicting Interests," read in part as follows:

> The seven Baby Bells, in one of the most dramatic indications yet of their conflicting interests, plan to sell off Bellcore, their jointly owned research arm formed in the breakup of the old AT&T empire a decade ago.
>
> The Bell regional operating companies are looking at offering Bell Communications Research for sale to the public in a stock offering, or perhaps selling a large chunk to a big strategic investor, selling the research unit outright on the open market, or utilizing a combination of those approaches, people close to the research lab said.[28]

The article went on to attribute the proposed sale to the intensification of competition among the RBOCs and with cable operators and long-distance carriers, and the RBOC's decreasing reliance on Bellcore as they built up their own R&D resources. It noted that US WEST, which could boast the most sophisticated research facility of the seven Baby Bells, was also one of the most vocal proponents of divestiture. Under these circumstances, Bellcore's relationship with its owners was changing. Increasingly, it was working with the RBOCs on a one-on-one basis. Finally, mention was made of Heilmeier's frustration in dealing with his client-owners. "If we had to get all seven companies to agree on technical programs, we'd sink to the lowest common denominator," he was quoted as saying.

On February 8, 1996, a landmark communications bill was signed into law by President Clinton. Passed a week earlier by both houses of Congress, by wide margins, the new legislation opened the gates for even greater rivalry in the telecommunications industry. The seven RBOCs could now offer long-distance phone service in competition with AT&T and each other. On their part, the RBOCs were required to open their local telephone networks to competitors, thus ending the long-held monopolies established by Judge Greene's decision in 1984. Cable television operators and telephone companies could attack each other with a full array of telephone, video, and high-speed data communications services.

A Commentary

Bellcore was formed in the context of a court judgment in an antitrust case. Four factors shaped its mission. First, it would serve as a pooled

R&D resource. Second, its membership would be limited to the seven newly formed Baby Bells. Third, like Bell Labs, it would rely on internal technology resources. And fourth, it was proscribed from working directly with the telecommunications industry's supply infrastructure in the design and fabrication of equipment. Unlike EPRI, SRC, GRI, and SEMATECH, but like MCC, which also relies on internal R&D, by far the greater part of Bellcore's agenda was devoted to elective work for individual members and member subsets. Thus, among the six consortia, all but MCC and Bellcore are focused primarily on a common R&D agenda and work extensively on supply infrastructure development.

There is a probable connection between the nature of a consortium's mission and its mode of R&D sourcing. Internal technical staff are likely to be perceived by member companies as resources to be drawn on to complement their own R&D programs. Consortia that rely on external sourcing and focus largely on infrastructure development may be valued more broadly, for industry development rather than for internal R&D. In the former case, contention may understandably erupt over how internal technology resources are to be shared among member companies. Contention may develop as well over the disposition of intellectual property, as it did at MCC. As member companies come to rely more on their own internal R&D, and as competition among them shrinks the scope of the R&D agenda on which they are willing to collaborate, consortial R&D may lose its relevance.

Moreover, members are likely to value collaborative enterprise differently, depending on the extent to which they have developed their own technology resources and the priority they give to the consortium's services. That is one way of explaining the friction among Bellcore's client-owners and the frustration of its leaders. Early in Bellcore's history Marano understood the importance of trust and patience to a successful tenure as Bellcore's CEO. And Heilmeier understood that he could not play favorites among members. Even so, the frustrations of leadership in Bellcore seem to exceed those in other consortia, except for MCC.

One cannot help but speculate on how Bellcore might have evolved had it been formed to represent the entire telecommunications industry and to focus on noncompetitive R&D, and had it not been precluded from working directly with the telecommunications supply industry. It might then have been able to adapt more readily to the industry's rapidly changing technical, regulatory, and competitive environment, and to the changing needs of its member companies. It might have been better positioned, as well, to pursue Heilmeier's vision of Bellcore as a key player in building a new information infrastructure.

VISION, MISSION, AND LEADERSHIP— A SYNTHESIS

Once again, the foundations of a successful consortium are a compelling vision, a viable and sustainable mission, and strong initial leadership. To attract support, a vision should articulate an important shared problem for which collective action promises an effective solution. Case histories suggest as well that a call to action carries weight only to the extent that it is identified with industry and/or government figures who are respected for their experience, accomplishments, and concern for their industry and/or country.

In its early stages, consortium formation and its mission may be only vaguely perceived, and there may be many ideas contributed by many interested parties. Thus moving beyond a vision to an achievable mission requires the selection of a clear and pragmatic objective, taking into account proposed funding levels, potential members' priorities, and relevant external constituencies' interests. A viable and sustainable mission has several attributes. First, it must not deal in areas of corporate core competencies, or threaten members' competitive advantage. Second, it must offer firm-specific economic value. Third, to the extent that it reflects public purpose and the national interest, a mission will have greater validity and legitimacy. But though collective or public purpose may attract support in the short run, in the long run the return to consortia members on their R&D investments becomes the more compelling motivation.

Vision

A vision may be the inspiration of business and/or government leaders, or both, as in the case of the Electric Power Research Institute. Joseph Swidler, chairman of the Federal Power Commission, was the first to articulate a need for an industry-wide R&D resource. Confirming voices came later from Senators Magnuson and Hollings and from Shearon Harris, presiding officer of the Edison Electric Institute. The idea of forming SEMATECH and the Semiconductor Research Corporation came out of board-level discussions in the Semiconductor Industry Association. A federal court gave birth to Bellcore. Government initiatives led to the development of numerous other R&D consortia in the United States, and to collaborative endeavors, such as VLSI and ICOT in Japan, and ESPRIT and EUREKA in Europe. (Japanese and European consortia are discussed in chapter 6.) In each instance the vision came with the voice of authority, whether of an industry statesperson, a court, the directors of an industry trade association, or a government funder.

In each case, too, the message was the need to cope with a widely shared problem which could be dealt with most effectively as a collaborative effort. SEMATECH, for example, provided an effective institutional solution for coping with the erosion of the domestic semiconductor manufacturing-equipment supply industry. While IBM or Intel or some other SEMA-TECH members might easily have funded the rebuilding of the supply infrastructure as a single-firm initiative, each gained economically by sharing the cost with other semiconductor manufacturers and users. Each one, and the federal government as well, had a significant stake in the viability of a domestic semiconductor manufacturing-equipment sector. The involvement of other industry members and the Department of Defense contributed to a successful outcome. As a collaborative effort, SEMATECH was also able to develop closer, more cost-efficient buyer-seller relationships in the vertical chain from equipment makers to semiconductor producers to chip users.

Sharing the benefits of infrastructure development among industry members did not come at a cost. Semiconductor manufacturing-equipment technology *per se* is not perceived as essential to the pursuit of competitive advantage at the chip-manufacturing level. To the contrary, it is to the advantage of semiconductor manufacturers to have an assured supply of standardized, state-of-the-art manufacturing equipment. Furthermore, any advance in semiconductor manufacturing equipment technology, however it were funded, would be difficult for any one firm to keep as proprietary knowledge.

Mission

Motivated by the need to form a collaborative venture that will generate the support of a substantial membership, promote a viable mission, and fulfill his or her personal concept of what a consortium should be, the founding CEO often plays a key role in the formulation of a mission. At SEMATECH, according to Larry Sumney, president of SRC, Robert Noyce "sorted through everything that had been proposed and picked the one thing to which SEMATECH could make a real contribution."[29]

At GRI, Dr. Henry Linden, GRI's founding CEO, shaped the consortium's mission in accordance with his own perception of the natural gas industry's needs. In June 1976, the Federal Power Commission envisioned a gas industry consortium that would address an "increasing imbalance between energy supply and demand," stating further: "We have not yet seen the level of concentrated and coordinated effort by the natural gas industry that the public interest requires to significantly advance the state of technology *to relieve the severe curtailment of service now being experienced by interstate natural gas pipelines.*"[30] [Emphasis added]

But Linden was convinced that a natural gas shortage was not the fundamental issue. According to him, "We were barking up the wrong tree. All of this work on finding natural gas substitutes was based on totally erroneous assessments of the gas resource base. We misled ourselves and the public into thinking that we would run out of natural gas."[31] Though Linden's conclusions were at odds with those of government and industry circles, which favored heavy investment in the development of coal gasification technology, in the early 1980s he moved to redefine GRI's mission, to stress "the development and commercialization of technologies that [could] retain and expand existing gas markets and develop new high form-value markets, all within the constraint of a least-cost energy service strategy."[32]

An important reason for giving greater priority to technology aimed at reducing the price of gas and improving its efficiency was GRI's need to gain concurrence from consumers and consumer advocacy groups, and from state and federal regulatory bodies. According to Linden:

> To do so, GRI had to justify its program as benefitting the consumer. It could clearly show how the consumer would benefit from lower costs and greater supply. A first big success was the pulse combustion furnace developed with Lennox. It improved gas burning efficiency from 50–60% to 95%. It was a roaring success.[33]

The focus now was on increasing the efficiency of gas to offset what had amounted to a 20 percent per year compound rate of escalation in its price, which had been associated with a drop in consumption from 22 tcf (trillion cubic feet) in 1973 to 16.2 tcf in 1986. The development of new gas-consuming products, such as a natural gas heat pump and natural gas vehicles, was one important objective. Another was to reduce the cost of producing and delivering gas in order to make it the least-cost energy source for consumers. A third was to increase the reliability (availability) of supply. In the past, supply uncertainty had inhibited market growth.

Also, at existing price levels, gas had been losing market share to electricity. By 1980, for example, the use of gas heating and cooling in new construction had plunged from 60 percent to about 30 percent.

In sum, unlike EPRI's mission, GRI's mission varied significantly from the original vision articulated by the Federal Power Commission. The FPC was particularly concerned about the impact that natural gas shortages were apparently having on interstate pipeline revenues, and wanted an industry-wide program to develop natural gas substitutes. Linden took exception to the FPC's definition of the problem, and focused instead on building an industry technology base and developing natural gas markets. Both Linden's own perception of industry needs, and perhaps more important, the need he recognized to serve GRI's multiple membership constituencies, led ultimately to a mission that gave priority to reducing gas prices and improving efficiency. Such an emphasis, by providing value for gas consumers, would generate the support of state regulatory bodies and consumer groups as well as of pipeline operators and local distribution companies. Thus GRI's mission, designed to appeal to its multiple membership and external constituencies, needed to do so in order to be viable.

Leadership

In the startup phase of a consortium, the founding CEO's tasks may include mission articulation, formulation of policies and strategies, establishment of governance structures and processes, development of funding sources, building a core membership group, recruiting competent technologists and staff, planning facilities, and gaining the support of external constituencies. And in all this, the perspectives of the initial visionaries and of the consortium's governing bodies must be taken into account.

What, then, would be the qualifications for leadership of an R&D consortium in the startup phase? While they may vary from one consortium to another, the following attributes are generally relevant. Ideally, a founding CEO might qualify as industry statesperson, having a reputation for integrity, fairness, and patience. Add to that administrative experience, negotiating skills, and the ability to establish network relationships in relevant circles. The desire to make a contribution may well be another requirement, not explicitly recognized in CEO selection. Indeed, a sense of wanting to make a difference and a need for career fulfillment are often a candidate's major personal reasons for taking on what is typically a very demanding assignment.

Leadership priorities for successive generations of consortia managers may vary somewhat from those of their predecessors, to reflect the fact that the consortium is by then an ongoing enterprise, well established as part of the R&D infrastructure, and that membership priorities have changed. Thus cost containment may loom large, as it did at Bellcore when Heilmeier succeeded Marano. The development of improved technology delivery systems may also be salient, as was the case when Steven Ban succeeded Henry Linden at GRI, and when Floyd Culler followed Chauncey Starr at EPRI. Other priorities may be the development of performance measures to quantify the value of consortium services to its members. William Spencer gave the development of such ROI measures high priority when he succeeded Robert Noyce at SEMATECH. Another priority may be the need to offer members more options in allocating their membership fees among various research areas, and between a common agenda and customized research—a need addressed by Richard Balzhiser when he became EPRI's CEO.

The point is, as consortia move through successive stages of growth, membership priorities shift, and the qualifications sought in their leadership change accordingly. Cost efficiency, performance measures, and improved technology delivery systems seem to gain in importance. Thus at Bellcore, MCC, and SEMATECH, the boards have turned to industry and government sources for managers who are bottom-line and market oriented. At GRI and EPRI, such qualifications were found in inside candidates.

Are the desired qualifications for consortium leadership different from those sought in corporate CEOs? That is not an easy question to answer, because in each domain the requirements of effective leadership vary considerably from one organization to another. Nevertheless, there are some differences. In particular, leadership of a consortium may require greater skill in coping with the demands of multiple external constituencies, as is demonstrated in the following chapter, on the politics of R&D planning. Internally, the consortium CEO may deal with the varied priorities of the directors who represent the consortium's membership constituencies—i.e., its customers. Unlike corporate boards, consortium boards are likely to be concerned primarily that the consortium meet the needs of their firms or the industry subsets they represent. In contrast, corporate boards, in theory at least, represent just one constituency—the shareholders. Their concerns are therefore growth and profitability. Thus, the consortium CEO must deal to a greater degree than his corporate counterparts with sometimes competing interests, both at the board and the committee or task force levels. The required skills may perhaps lie more in the art of negotiation and consensus-building than might be the case in private enterprise. Internally as well, the consortium CEO is called on to mediate the respective interests and values of the organization's technical personnel, business-oriented managers, and membership representatives.

Finally, CEOs in the two domains may differ in their career incentives. In the author's experience, private-sector CEOs are prone to measure success in terms of market share, stockholder value, and their own compensation. In comparison, their consortia counterparts—at least those who lead the collaborative ventures described in this study—seem more concerned with the opportunity to lead organizations with the potential for making a significant contribution to the advance of technology and economic growth. Chauncey Starr, EPRI's founding CEO, recalled, "I had no particular reason to want to leave UCLA. But maybe EPRI might give me an opportunity for making a greater contribution. That was what my wife and I talked about. My idea was to develop EPRI as a mainstream vehicle for helping society."[34]

Similarly, George Heilmeier, Bellcore's second CEO, saw Bellcore as a key player in the building of a new information infrastructure comparable historically to the development of the shipping, canal, road, railroad, and air transport systems. He wanted Bellcore to be the architect of the coming Information Superhighway.[35] And Robert Noyce, who chaired the selection committee for SEMATECH's CEO, reluctantly accepted its call after a long and unsuccessful search, opining that he was too old for the job. Noyce's acceptance could only have been motivated by a sense of personal commitment to SEMATECH's mission and to the U.S. semiconductor industry at large.

Like Starr, Heilmeier, and Noyce, many R&D consortium leaders are in the later stages of their careers. Job advancement and income are probably not major incentives for taking on the management of organizations with a broad range of internal and external constituencies. They are drawn instead by a sense of personal mission.

IN SUMMARY

The foundations of a successful consortium are a compelling vision, a viable and sustainable mission, and strong initial leadership. To attract support, the vision should articulate an important shared problem for which collective action promises the most efficient and effective solution. Case histories suggest as well that a call to action carries weight to the extent that it is identified with industry or government figures respected for their experience, accomplishments, and broad concern for their industries. At this stage the specific mission a proposed collective endeavor might pursue may not be clear, and a plethora of ideas may emanate from a range of interested parties. Moving from a vision to the formulation of a policy and strategy requires a mission orientation—something that is doable given the proposed level of funding, the priorities of potential members, and the interests of relevant external constituencies. Ultimately the mission is often clarified and articulated by the founding CEO.

A viable mission has several characteristics. First, it must not deal in domains of corporate core competencies or threaten consortium members' competitive advantages. Second, it must offer firm-specific economic value. To the extent that a consortium reflects public purpose and the national interest, it will have validity and legitimacy. As a primary mission, however, collective or public purpose may attract support only in the short run. In the long run, return on R&D investments becomes the more compelling objective—and at least in the United States, that measure tends to give priority to short-term results. Ultimately, the original mission may lose relevance as competitive factors change and technology advances. At that point, the key to survival is likely to be reformulating the mission to serve more effectively the evolving needs of the membership.

CHAPTER 3

The Politics of R&D Planning

R&D planning is essentially a politically driven process for allocating a pool of funds among competing constituency interests. In addition to consortium members, the constituency set may include government funders, regulatory agencies, Congress, consumer and public interest groups, and consortium managers. The political intensity and complexity of the planning process tends to vary with the diversity of membership subgroups, the range and sensitivity of external stakeholders, the industry's regulatory environment, and the competitive milieu. For example, R&D planning is far more politically driven at GRI than at SEMATECH. Among the six consortia examined in this book, GRI has the most diverse membership, plus a wide range of external stakeholders and an R&D agenda that spans all aspects of natural gas industry technology. In addition, GRI falls under the jurisdiction of the Federal Energy Regulatory Commission (FERC), which has ultimate control over the size of its R&D budget, and approval authority for the scope and content of its R&D program.

In comparison, SEMATECH's membership consists only of large firms in the computer and semiconductor industries, drawn together for a single purpose: strengthening the U.S. semiconductor equipment manufacturing industry. With half of SEMATECH's funding coming from the U.S. defense establishment, and with the industry's Roadmap for long-range planning, R&D planning is essentially a priority-setting process—a matter of advancing technology along a predetermined path, toward a commonly established goal. Regulatory influence is not a factor, nor do other external interests shape SEMATECH's planning. Accordingly, R&D planning is considerably less politicized at SEMATECH than at GRI.

Contention among interested parties regarding R&D planning generally centers on the three basic parameters of the R&D program: the size of the overall budget, the technology domains the consortium will explore, and the allocation of funds—to broad areas, particular projects, and work for the membership body as a whole or for individual members and member subsets.

THE BASIC R&D PLANNING PROCESS

In its simplest form, the planning of the common R&D agenda is a top-down, bottom up iterative process. At the board level, decisions are made about the allocation of funds among broad research areas. Working within those parameters, task forces consisting of member company representatives and consortium personnel develop R&D program proposals for review at higher levels, and ultimately for approval by the board.

The basic annual planning process at SRC is representative of planning at all six consortia. Involved in it are SRC's board of directors; the Executive Technical Advisory Board (ETAB), composed largely of member-company research directors; six Technical Advisory Boards (TABs), all composed of other member-company representatives; and an internal Research Management Committee (RMC). The research planning process is iterative. The board first determines the scientific areas[1] on which SRC will focus and establishes a preliminary allocation of funds across those areas, taking into account the recommendations of ETAB and SRC's staff. The TABs develop program proposals for their respective technical fields, working from several data sources. The first source is the Mission and Outlook statement, prepared by SRC's vice president and chief scientist. It describes the current state of technology and outlines industry trends, the government environment, and SRC's revenue forecasts. TAB members also have information on research contracts in progress and proposed new projects in their respective areas, as well as knowledge of their own companies' research needs. Working from these data, they develop prioritized lists of projects for SRC funding.

These lists are submitted to the ETAB for review and then returned to the TABs, with cutoff points set by ETAB-established funding limits. The TABs might then review and revise their program proposals, working within their research budgets. The planning process is carried out with the aid of a computerized decision-support program, to enable the TABs and the ETAB members to review and work through different iterations by project time horizons, science areas, university affiliation, and research thrust, among other factors. Finally, the ETAB then submits the proposed program to the SRC staff, which seeks approval from SRC's board. As described by Dr. Daniel Fleming, SRC board chairman:

> The ETAB acts as an impedance match between the technology people and the more business-oriented people at the board level. Its job is to convince the board that the program is in balance and, on the other end, to help the technical people in the TABs to understand why the board makes the decisions it makes.[2]

Dr. Court Skinner, an ETAB member, commented: "The ETAB is only an advisory body to the board and the SRC management. But if we're upset, they listen. They like to have our recommendations before they make a decision."[3]

The R&D committee structure, involving large numbers of member-company representatives, is the primary vehicle for member-company input to the planning process. It serves to educate member-company personnel on advances in technology and to give them a sense of ownership in the consortium.

As noted, agenda-setting processes such as this one typify the planning of the consortium's common agenda. In contrast, projects that are carried out for individual members and groups of members, as at EPRI, Bellcore, and MCC, are typically negotiated between the member set and consortium personnel. Often they are initiated by consortium technical personnel and member-company representatives, with additional member sponsors sometimes solicited by consortium personnel to secure a critical mass of funding.

THE POLITICS OF R&D PLANNING AT GRI

At GRI, R&D planning is also top-down, bottom-up, but the process is considerably more politicized than it is at SRC. Three factors have a significant influence on the size of the R&D budget, its allocation among technology areas, and the domains in which GRI may work and those which are off-limits. One factor is the diversity of GRI's membership. Another is GRI's oversight by a government agency, the Federal Energy Regulatory Commission. A third is the fact that the broad parameters of GRI's overall program—the size of its budget, its R&D objectives, and its funding sources—are routinely challenged by outside interest groups. We will consider each of these factors in turn.

Membership Diversity

Internally, the most critical planning decision at GRI is the allocation of funds among its four major areas of research and development. They are:

- supply options (R&D focused on the development of natural gas supplies at optimal costs, to meet long-term demand);
- gas operations (technology aimed at achieving safe, low-cost, environmentally sound gas transmission, storage, and distribution);
- end uses (the development of safe, environmentally sound, and economically viable value-added end use applications to benefit the consumer and the gas industry);
- cross-cutting (otherwise uncategorized) R&D aimed at providing new technologies for natural gas production, transport, and use, and at meeting environmental and safety regulations).

Each of GRI's several membership subsets—the gas producers, the interstate pipelines, and the local distribution companies—tends to favor a different research area. Each subset holds six seats on GRI's board of directors. Three more directors represent major gas-consuming companies. And three board members come from GRI's advisory council, which includes nine state utility commissioners as well as representatives of such external constituencies as the academic community, environmentalists, the scientific and engineering community, the legal and regulatory fields, and labor. Thus the advisory council's three representatives on the board give voice to a wide range of stakeholders.

Other inputs to the planning process come from three other bodies that act in an advisory capacity to the board. The Industry Technical Advisory Committee (ITAC) includes members from trade associations representing gas and oil producers, gas pipelines, and gas appliance manufacturers, as well as some members drawn directly from the interstate pipelines, gas producers, and local distribution companies. ITAC's role is to review the overall R&D budget, the balance among the four main research areas, and the strategies and goals of each program area, and to make recommendations on those matters to the board.

The Research Coordination Council (RCC) represents major academic, private, and federal institutions involved in energy research. It reviews the technical adequacy, relevance, and likelihood of success of R&D efforts, notes efforts that may be complementary or duplicative, and recommends areas for collaboration. The Municipal Gas System Advisory Committee (MUGSAC), formed in 1978 at the urging of state regulatory commissions, provides guidance from the perspective of the municipal utilities and their customers, and makes relevant recommendations. Finally, the Department of Energy (DOE) is particularly influential in GRI's R&D planning, and is represented on the RCC. The DOE and GRI have negotiated joint research agreements, and they jointly fund specific R&D programs.

From GRI's founding in 1979 through 1994, allocation of funds among the four R&D areas has evolved markedly, influenced both by national priorities and by individual constituency interests. Because of early public concern about natural gas supply, 57 percent of GRI's budget for 1979 was committed to technological development of supply options. That figure declined to a low of 25.7 percent in 1988, then rose to 31 percent in 1994, following the addition of board seats for the gas-producer segment of the industry. End-use R&D went from 27.3 percent of the budget in 1979 to 48.6 percent in 1994, reflecting the interest of local distribution companies in growing the natural-gas share of the U.S. energy market. While R&D on gas operations has grown from 4.7 percent of the 1979 budget to 19.3 percent of the 1994 budget, it is still relatively small compared to research on supply options and end uses—despite the fact that GRI was conceived to support that segment of the industry, and that interstate pipelines provide the bulk of GRI's funding. Finally, cross-cutting research dropped from 11 percent of the 1979 budget to a minuscule 1.1 percent in 1994. Projects that fall into that category seem now to have little constituency support, and/or there seems to be no real interest in undertaking long-term R&D aimed at breakthrough technological advances.

Though R&D allocations should be expected to shift over time as technology evolves, in GRI's case, they seem to reflect a shift in the balance of representation on governance bodies. In the interplay of constituency interests, funding for breakthrough technologies and for environmental health and safety has been considerably diminished.

Role of the Federal Energy Regulatory Commission (FERC)

By law, the Federal Energy Regulatory Commission has jurisdiction over the interstate gas pipeline and, accordingly, over GRI, since the consortium is funded largely by a surcharge levied on the interstates, based on their throughput volume. In 1977, when GRI was formed, the Commission asserted its authority over the consortium's R&D expenditures in FERC Order 566, which established the procedures by which annual funding applications would be made. Drafted after GRI filed its first application for funding with FERC in 1977, and agreed to by GRI and FERC with later amendments, this set of stipulations spelled out in some detail guidelines for FERC's oversight. It dealt with the standards by which individual projects would be judged, budget restrictions, mandated funding sources, and other matters.[4]

GRI is required to submit annually its R&D plan for the coming year, including detailed information on each R&D project: those in progress, those completed or dropped, and proposed new initiatives. The stipulations also require the inclusion of cost-benefit analyses for all projects and priority rankings. "An objective of future programming and funding," the agreement notes, "shall be to move high priority new technology into use for the benefit of pipeline gas ratepayers in the shortest practical time."

The stipulations also provide dollar and percentage limits on project overruns, and require that documentation be submitted to FERC explaining any changes from approved plans. Overall, expenditures in each program area must be kept within budget unless a deviation is approved by FERC in response to a written request from GRI. With regard to funding, GRI agreed that it would use its best efforts to secure cofunding from firms it awarded R&D contracts. It further agreed to treat all revenues received through royalties from patents, licenses, the sale of assets, and interest accrued on unspent funds as credits against future budgets.

Another provision was that "GRI will serve its future applications [for funding] on all of its members and state commissions, and there will be public notice with opportunities for comments." In addition, GRI's officers promised to recommend to the board of directors that five representatives of state regulatory commissions be given seats on the Advisory Council, and that one should be named Council chairperson and be invited to attend all board meetings.

Such conditions as these give FERC considerable power and influence over GRI. FERC controls GRI's funding, establishes its R&D priorities and objectives, circumscribes its project planning, and orchestrates other inputs to the planning process, both external and internal. FERC's requirements have added significantly to GRI's costs. In GRI's 1993 filing it noted that reporting costs were escalating as the result of "new legal and regulatory requirements," and that FERC staff and advisors were "asking increasingly detailed questions about individual GRI activities." Requesting relief, GRI's management petitioned FERC in 1993 to go from a one-year to a two-year planning cycle.

The current planning cycle provided for three reviews annually of each of the major components of GRI's RD&D program, which were intended to justify the direction and budget for each project—even those that were FERC-approved—and to establish that work was continuing on schedule and within budget.[5] Under the proposed planning format, year-by-year project plans would be replaced with plans describing the full cycle of RD&D, the commercialization steps necessary to deliver proposed products, and the anticipated ratepayer and industry benefits. Two-year detailed program budgets would be filed with FERC, with abbreviated filings in intervening years. The abbreviated filings would deal with proposed budget adjustments and with new project proposals. The anticipated benefits of the new planning approach included a reduction of ten to fifteen person-years over the two-year cycle and a savings of $2 million annually in contracts for outside planning and analytical services.

External Interest Groups

A wide range of stakeholders contribute to reviews of GRI's submissions to FERC. They include state utility commissions, federal agencies, the National Association of Regulated Utility Commissions, the oil pipelines, gas utilities, and oil and gas producers. Among these, the Process Gas Consumers Group (PGC), representing large industrial gas consumers, is one of the most active.[6] In 1989 and again in 1991, PGC brought suits, known as "PGC I" and "PGC II," against FERC in the U.S. Circuit Court of Appeals, District of Columbia.[7] PGC's fundamental objective was to hold down the price of gas paid by industrial end-users. Thus it sought to proscribe GRI from doing end-use research that might increase the demand for and the price of natural gas. Then, to limit the impact on gas prices of funding the GRI program (at that time 1.51 cents per mcf), PGC pressed for three concessions: a dollar cap on GRI's FERC-approved budget, mandatory minimum levels of cofunding by GRI's commercial partners, and greater reliance on royalty income and low-interest loans in funding GRI's programs.

In PGC I, the plaintiffs argued that under the Natural Gas Policy Act of 1978, FERC's jurisdiction was limited to the approval of research related to the "production, transportation, and sale of natural gas in interstate commerce," not end-use research. But the court found that construct "unduly restrictive" and ruled that "FERC, consistent with the Natural Gas Act, may authorize ratepayer financing of end-item research that has as its 'broad goal' the purpose of 'keeping consumer rates down.' "

The court did agree, however, that GRI's end-use R&D should be limited to projects of primary benefit to *existing* classes of ratepayers, as opposed to the development of new consumer markets. The court observed further that end-use research "aimed at generating *new* demand for natural gas" was likely to increase the demand for and the price of gas. Such research was less likely to have "a reasonable chance of benefiting the ratepayer in a reasonable period of time," as required by FERC regulations.

The court then went on to establish what became known as a net benefits test, by which each proposed end-use project would be evaluated in terms of (1) the net present value (NPV) of the economic benefits that would accrue to *existing* classes of ratepayers through consumer savings, plus (2) any savings in transportation and distribution costs; less (3) R&D costs to project completion and (4) the NPV of increased costs to existing ratepayers due to gas price increases resulting from increased demand, as users of other forms of energy switched to gas.

Following the trials, the cases were remanded to FERC for settlement under court-established guidelines. FERC subsequently promulgated Opinion 378 (November 1992), which outlined the terms of a settlement. The provisions of Opinion 378 were mandated in FERC's order of March 22, 1993, the so-called Stipulation and Agreement of 1993. GRI incurred substantial legal fees to fight PGC's initiatives.

Pursuant to the court's judgment in PGC1, FERC adopted a taxonomy proposed by GRI to conform to the court's ruling. It distinguished among three classes of research projects, as follows. Class 1 research would include those projects the benefits of which would accrue exclusively to existing classes of ratepayers, and which would generate very little new demand. For example, R&D projects aimed at developing more efficient residential and commercial gas appliances and advanced industrial heat-transfer systems would fall into Class 1.

Class 2 research, while conducted for the primary benefit of current gas consumers, might also create add-on uses. If it could be demonstrated that Class 2 research would *predominantly* benefit existing classes of ratepayers, although attracting "fuel-switchers," it could pass the net benefits test. One example of this class of technology would be gas-powered residential cooling as an added option for customers already using gas for space-heating, water-heating, clothes-drying, and/or cooking.

Class 3 technologies would create new uses for natural gas, and would not qualify for GRI funding. By their nature, benefits from Class 3 research would not be limited to existing classes of ratepayers, and might be of substantial benefit to new classes of consumers, e.g., vehicular transportation.

Two Class 3 projects approved earlier by FERC, but found by the court to be inconsistent with its ruling in the first case, were the natural gas vehicle project and the natural gas emission-control project.[8] Following the court's decision in the second case, however, Congress passed Public Law 102-104 and the Energy Policy Act of 1992, which effectively overturned the ruling. Under the new legislation, FERC was authorized to approve R&D funding for such projects if it found that "the benefits, including environmental benefits, to both existing and future ratepayers resulting from such activities exceed all direct costs to both existing and future ratepayers."[9] FERC then reviewed GRI's natural gas vehicles and emission-control projects and found that their cost/benefit ratios were sufficiently favorable even without taking into account environmental benefits to justify the continuation of both projects.

PGC successfully achieved its other objectives. In the negotiations following the court hearings, GRI agreed to both mandatory cofunding and a 1994 budget cap of $201.8 million.[10] In return, the Industrial Groups agreed to withdraw five pending lawsuits that contested FERC approval of GRI's programs for 1988 through 1992. In addition, they agreed not to challenge the federal legislation which had allowed FERC to approve GRI's R&D programs for natural gas vehicles and emissions control. Finally, pursuant to the settlements in PGC I and II, the large industrial gas users were granted three seats on GRI's board of directors.

Elizabeth Anne Molar, one of the five FERC commissioners, filed a dissenting opinion expressing her dissatisfaction with GRI's budget cap. She stated her strong belief that limiting GRI's growth was not in the public interest. Both the Department of Energy and the Environmental Protection Agency, she noted, had stressed the importance of GRI's work in support of a national energy strategy and environmental goals. She reminded the commissioners that following FERC's approval of GRI's 1992 budget, they had asked GRI to consider expanding its R&D budget. Molar concluded:

> GRI has faced a formidable opponent in its litigation with PGC. The Commission has supported GRI's efforts over the years in that litigation. Congress has gone to great lengths to support the GRI R&D program. In response to the PGC I case, the court has reaffirmed the GRI program in the PGC II case. *Yet, sadly, GRI has thrown in the towel at a time when this Nation needs an enhanced*

R&D program, not a moribund one. As far as I am concerned, this is a case of lost opportunity. [Emphasis added]

SOME OBSERVATIONS

Of the six consortia, GRI is the most prone to politicized decision making in such broad and important domains as budget levels, the allocation of funds among research areas, and project qualification requirements.[11] Contention on these matters may be attributed to four conditions:

- built-in ambiguity with regard to who is GRI's customer;
- a membership composed of multiple constituencies with divergent priorities;
- a plethora of external constituencies, with differing degrees of power to intervene in decision making;
- tight governmental monitoring and regulation with respect to program funding amounts and sources, program content, and reporting procedures.

Who Is the Customer?

Established originally to address the plight of the interstate pipelines, resulting from dwindling pipeline throughput during the gas shortages of the 1970s, GRI was quickly charged with serving all segments of the gas industry. But to qualify for FERC approval, GRI's R&D projects had to promise benefits to ratepayers—a rule that established the consumer as the ultimate customer. The end-customer became even more narrowly defined, as *existing* classes of ratepayers, pursuant to legal actions brought in PGC I and PGC II.

The interests of existing classes of ratepayers are favored in GRI's R&D planning through the application of the net-benefits tests just described. In addition, state public utility commissions, strongly represented in GRI's governance structure, are likely to weigh in on the side of consumer interests. The supporting rationale for this bias is that because the cost of GRI's program is borne by existing ratepayers, the consortium's work must be limited to projects primarily for their benefit. But consortia that serve unregulated industries are not so bound. And indeed, to argue that private corporations should direct business development initiatives solely at those currently buying its products would be quite inconsistent with stockholder interests, as well as the interests of the economy as a whole. Thus if the priority accorded to the interests of existing ratepayers precludes the development of new applications and new markets for natural gas, it may come at some long-run cost to the gas industry and potential future gas users. In sum, GRI seems doomed to serve two masters, with existing classes of ratepayers receiving priority.

Membership Diversity

GRI's membership is vertically structured, representing as it does all segments of the gas industry—production, transportation, and distribution—in accordance with its articles of incorporation. Contention arises, then, over how some finite pool of R&D funding is to be divided in accordance with its several R&D priorities. Contention develops too over how the funding burden is to be divided among vertically related industry segments. While in theory the interstate pipelines "write the checks" for R&D and pass the charge on to ratepayers, each industry segment claims that GRI funding comes largely (and unfairly) off its own bottom line.

The FERC-mediated negotiations of 1991 to 1992, which led to revisions in the R&D funding formula, were a prolonged and agonizing effort to readjust the funding burden.[12] They were precipitated by allegations by the interstate pipeline operators, that they were not able to pass the R&D surcharge of 1.51 cents per mcf up the line to the local distribution companies. In fact, two major interstate pipelines, ANR Pipeline and United Gas Pipelines, resigned over the issue in 1991 and 1992.

At GRI, the conflict over who pays how much is a manifestation of a contention that normally exists among firms that are related as buyers and sellers in a value chain going from raw materials to end-products. The question is how industry profits are to be shared at different levels. In general, value-chain profit allocations are worked out through pricing and cost-transfer mechanisms. Internalizing such a contention within a consortium, however, simply increases the politicization of decision making. In horizontally structured consortia, contention of this sort is not evident.

External Stakeholder Intervention

As noted, GRI's external constituencies include government agencies such as DOE and EPA, state public utility commissions, trade associations, gas appliance manufacturers, environmental groups, and residential and industrial users. These groups are given a voice in GRI governance through their representation on advisory councils and their right to intervene in GRI's annual plan review and FERC's approval process.

Having to deal with a plethora of stakeholders must be accepted as a fact of life for consortia such as GRI, operating in the vortex of public and private interests. At issue is the degree of power some constituencies wield relative to others. In particular, the economic clout of the large industrial gas users represented by PGC has been used effectively to limit, at least temporarily, any growth in GRI's program, and to rule out any R&D initiatives beyond those of benefit to existing classes of ratepayers. By arguing against any end-product research, as well as research not intended primarily to benefit existing classes of ratepayers, PGC in effect sought to limit GRI's potential contribution to the natural gas industry and to economic development. Thus, in PGC I and II and in pursuant negotiations, PGC was seeking to advance its members' interests over such national priorities as emissions control and the development of gas-powered vehicles. PGC was successful in doing so until its efforts were overridden by acts of Congress.

Regulatory Influence

Regulation of GRI comes in the form of excessively detailed orders and stipulations governing reporting requirements, the program approval process, project qualification standards, funding sources and amounts, budget overrun limits, and the composition of GRI's governance bodies. FERC mandates strongly shape GRI's R&D strategy and governance, and impose heavy costs in personnel, time, and money. Thus, without judging the merit of FERC-imposed requirements, it may be said that GRI's direction is necessarily formulated within bounds established by FERC, and that such regulation contributes to the politicization of the planning process.

The factors that determine the balance of constituency power at GRI were in place at the outset. That is, the consortium comes under regulatory control; it has a diverse membership; and one membership constituency, the interstate pipelines, underwrites the entire R&D program. These factors set the stage for contention, serving ultimately to enhance the power of external stakeholders in shaping GRI's governance structure and the scope of its technology program, funding levels, and R&D planning. FERC itself has a significant influence on GRI in all these respects, and in the exercise of its authority, it has encouraged the intervention of external interest groups. In fact, FERC has become a leverage point for the exercise of power by such outside constituencies as the PGC.

The original funding scheme, in which the interstate pipelines "write the check" for GRI's R&D program, has created dissension among the consortium's internal and external stakeholders. This scheme appears to have been conceived when GRI's mission was to reverse the decline in pipeline throughput attributed to natural gas shortages. In that version of GRI's mission, the interstates would have been GRI's primary client. But the present funding arrangement seems anachronistic given that GRI's mandate is to serve all segments of the gas industry.

A TYPOLOGY OF CONSTITUENCY POWER

To a significant extent, R&D consortium management is constituency management. While few consortia may have GRI's plethora of stakeholders, all must deal with some range of external and internal interest groups. Thus four sources of power come to bear on decisions regarding membership, funding, governance structures and processes, and planning of the R&D agenda. They are market-derived, right of governance, legal and jurisdictional power, and right of representation.

The first category, *market-derived power,* accrues to those groups that are in one way or another the consortium's clients—that is, its members and other funders. Among these, the larger members have proportionally greater influence, particularly in R&D planning, because they are often better represented in the top governance bodies and on operating task forces than the smaller members. Large companies also have greater power of defection. If they withdraw or threaten to do so, their action may not only reduce consortium revenues, but more important, it may start a chain reaction of withdrawals. Thus GRI moved quickly to renegotiate the funding formula with the several interested parties when two major interstate pipelines resigned from membership in 1991 and 1992, raising the specter that others would follow suit.

Governance power is held by those elected and appointed to consortia boards of directors, advisory committees, and management positions. Directors serve at the sufferance of the membership constituencies they represent, and have the authority to establish policy, elect members of top management, and review and approve consortium strategy. Members of consortium management gain power initially through the authority granted to them, enhanced by whatever experience and prestige they bring to their work. Their power is augmented as well by their inside knowledge of consortium operations; their network relationships with both internal and external constituencies; their reputations for integrity and fairness; and their competence as managers. They exercise the power of initiative in such matters as recommendations for board and committee appointments, overall R&D strategy, new R&D programs, and organizational innovations.

Legal and jurisdictional power resides with the courts, legislative bodies, and federal and state regulatory agencies, which by law may have the right to exert authority over any or all aspects of consortium policy and operations. In the case of GRI, the Federal Energy Regulatory Commission is the dominant regulatory power. At EPRI, the state public utility commissions constitute the principal regulatory influence. In both cases, the commissions' ultimate authority comes through their power to approve consortium funding. Congress as well may intervene to exercise its authority, both in favor of the public interest and against the power of other constituencies.

Rights of representation belong to those outside constituencies which may be affected by consortium priorities, decisions, and actions. At GRI, many of these stakeholders participate in an advisory capacity, both to the board and to management, as members of councils and committees. They have no voting power; typically they derive their power from the external stakeholders they represent, and from their positions in the broader scientific and public interest communities. They also bestow legitimacy, in the sense that they may accept or reject the consortium's purposes and programs as valid in that broader context.

Among those not already represented on advisory councils are stakeholders such as consumer advocacy groups and some trade associations. They may have a voice through jurisdictional proceedings, such as those conducted by FERC with regard to GRI's annual filings. Or they may assert their rights and interests through political actions targeted at bodies with legal power, such as the state public utility commissions and the courts. An example is the Process Gas Consumers Group and other industry associations.

CONCLUSIONS

At the heart of a consortium's strategy is its R&D program. Accordingly, R&D planning processes are critical. They should provide orderly ways of generating and screening a range of project proposals and of selecting from among them in accordance with cost-benefit measures and the negotiated priorities of the consortium's membership. But with the several interested parties contending over budget size, scope of R&D, and the allocation of funds, the process can become politicized. The degree of contention is affected by three factors: the scope of the consortium's R&D program, the extent of divergence among membership constituency interests, and the power of external constituencies to influence R&D program priorities.

What may be concluded from GRI's experience under regulation? First, meeting the requirements imposed under regulation can be onerous, costly, and time consuming. Second, the regulatory body may become a lightning rod for the intervention of external constituencies in pursuit of their own self-interest. The more powerful may be able to set the broad parameters of consortium operations, and in doing so may preempt other interests. Third, regulatory bodies tend to assert their own priorities. One effect of regulatory influence on R&D planning at GRI has been to establish the primacy of existing end-users—ratepayers—as the market the consortium serves, rather than of member companies per se. The underlying rationale is that ultimately the current consumer pays for GRI's R&D program, so the current consumer should therefore be the beneficiary. But consortia in unregulated industries are under no such restrictions in establishing their priorities. Their R&D expenditures are considered investments in their members' future growth and profitability. Would regulated enterprise—and the national economy as well—not be better served through the development of new markets than through a commitment to serving only existing customer sets? In this context regulators align, it seems, with the perceived short-term interests of current consumers, not with the long-run best interests of future consumers and of the industries consortia are formed to serve.

In the author's opinion, consortium regulation is not likely to serve the best interests of the consortium's member companies and other stakeholders. As a matter of public policy, the current wave of deregulation in such sectors as energy and telecommunications might well be extended to the R&D consortia that serve those industries. To do so would help to focus consortia missions, reduce administrative costs, and allow collaborative enterprises to grow or decline to the extent that they serve a market need for new technologies.

Going beyond consortia that serve regulated industries, what may be said about the challenges of coping with multiple internal and external constituencies? First, GRI's travails underscore the need for a cohesive membership and a clear and unambiguous mission. Second, R&D governance structures and processes might well be designed to give primary power and influence to the consortia membership. R&D planning initiatives and choices at all governance levels are the legitimate domain of the consortium's client-owners. Over the long run, the sustainability of a mission depends on how effectively a consortium responds to their market-derived power.

Third, rights of representation and the input of external stakeholders should be respected for what they can contribute to the consortium's direction and to its legitimacy within the technical, economic, social, and political milieu in which it operates. Such input may be most constructive if given as advisories. To give voting power to external stakeholders, however, may serve only to escalate the degree of internal tension in consortium governance.

Finally, what if a consortium is subjected to legal and jurisdictional forces that impact its objectives and its R&D program? Perhaps the only viable strategy is to work to build supportive and mutually beneficial relationships with such external power sources. It may well serve a consortium's interests, as well, to develop the support of other influential external constituencies, as GRI has done with DOE and EPA. To a greater or lesser extent, constituency management is basically an exercise in institutional politics.

CHAPTER 4

Consortium Strategy

An R&D consortium exists to produce and deliver a range of services to a defined member set, in exchange for revenues derived through some established schedule of fees. Thus the basic elements of a consortium's strategy are (1) its membership constituency, as well as other funders (that is, the markets it will serve); (2) its R&D sourcing modes (basically the choice between an internal staff and external contracting); (3) its product line, or the range of services it will provide; (4) its pricing modes (that is, the forms in which its revenues are derived—e.g., one-time shareholder fees, annual membership dues, cost-per-project charges); and (5) its R&D delivery systems (the channels used in the diffusion of new technology to member companies, their suppliers, and their markets). These five elements of strategy are the ongoing concern of consortia boards of directors and managers. They warrant continuing reexamination and often reformulation as technology moves ahead, member-company priorities change, and an industry's competitive milieu evolves. In this chapter, we consider the options for consortia governance related to each of these five elements, and the factors that condition strategic choice.

MEMBERSHIP COMPOSITION

A consortium's mission and the makeup of its membership are of course inextricably linked. Bellcore was established to advance telecommunications technology exclusively for the seven Baby Bells. EPRI was formed to conduct R&D for the electric power industry. SEMATECH's mission is to help maintain U.S. supremacy in the semiconductor industry, and in particular to strengthen the domestic manufacturing-equipment infrastructure. Its members are the major U.S. producers and consumers of semiconductors.

Four basic issues are relevant in establishing a consortium's membership policy, both at its formation and later, as the technical, competitive, and political environments in which the consortium operates change. First is the matter of *exclusivity.* Under what conditions should some potential membership sets be excluded? What are the benefits and costs of exclusivity? Second is the relative degree of *member cohesiveness* around common R&D needs and priorities. Members of consortia that are not focused on some temporary, narrowly defined R&D task will vary with regard to what they want from the consortium. To a great extent, such diversity may be coped with through consensus-building processes for R&D planning and an array of product/price options. At some point, however, differences may be so great as to fragment the R&D program, making it difficult to satisfy the needs of the entire membership.

The third issue is the matter of *membership structure.* What are the advantages of vertical composition—that is, of bringing buyers and their suppliers together in a collaborative venture—as opposed to horizontal composition—that is, of limiting membership to one particular level in the value chain. GRI, for example, is a vertically structured consortium, with a membership that is representative of gas producers, pipelines, and local distribution companies. Bellcore's membership is organized horizontally.

Finally, how do consortia take account of *free riders* in shaping their membership policies? Free riders are nonmember firms that have access to a consortium's output. Without paying membership fees, they gain the benefits of consortium R&D through papers published in scientific journals, the commercialization of new technical advances by R&D contractors, and growth in the markets they serve generated by consortium-developed products and services. We will consider each of these issues in the discussion that follows.

Exclusivity

Exclusionary policies arise largely out of concern for competitive advantage. Thus consortia that are formed to advance the interests of domestic industries in global competition (such as SEMATECH and SRC) may explicitly exclude foreign companies from membership. The exclusivity issue arises as well with regard to competitors in domestic markets. For example, should EPRI, formed originally to serve regulated electric utilities, offer membership to unregulated, independent power producers (IPPs), which compete aggressively for a share of the electric power market? Should Bellcore, with only the seven RBOCs as members, open its doors to the plethora of telephone companies, both large and small, in the United States or the world?

Typically, such exclusions go back to the consortium's raison d'être. Both MCC and SEMATECH were formed in direct response to Japan's ascendancy in the world markets for semiconductors, computers, and semiconductor manufacturing equipment. Both were established with the full support of Congress and government agencies, concerned about the effects on the U.S. economy and U.S. military preparedness of the loss of the semiconductor market to the Japanese. Moreover, SEMATECH received half its funding—$100 million a year for five years—from the Department of Defense. Accordingly, there was good reason to exclude foreign firms from membership in SEMATECH.

For both MCC and SEMATECH, the cause became part of the culture. At SEMATECH in particular, founding CEO Robert Noyce frequently reminded the consortium's members and personnel that they were engaged in an economic war against Japan. The headquarters building was decorated in red, white, and blue, with photographs of semiconductors on which American flags had been superimposed. Luncheon speakers were called in to address SEMATECH employees on the seriousness of yielding supremacy in semiconductors to "Japan, Inc."

Four points may be made with regard to exclusionary membership provisions. First, members may vary in their support of such restrictions. Second, excluding foreign companies from U.S. consortia may have a reciprocal effect; consortia based in other countries have barred U.S. firms from membership in retaliation. Third, excluding certain classes of firms from membership may not preclude their access to the consortium's output. And fourth, exclusions may remain in force as vestigial elements of a consortium's culture and/or as a condition of funding support—say, in SEMATECH's case—from the government.

On the first point, as the Japanese threat receded and the U.S. began to regain market share in computers, semiconductors, and semiconductor manufacturing equipment, IBM became less supportive of barring foreign firms from admission to SEMATECH. John Armstrong, for one, thought the idea was "preposterous," observing that because SEMATECH membership was limited to U.S. firms, IBM had not been allowed to join the Joint European Submicron Silicon Institute (JESSI).[1] Other SEMATECH members with a greater concentration of operations in the United States might favor the retention of membership restrictions.

As for precluding access to consortium output, SEMATECH made no move—nor could it—to restrict where and to whom U.S. semiconductor equipment manufacturers could sell. In fact, about half the equipment market was outside the United States, mostly in Japan. Accordingly, U.S. chip manufacturers' foreign competitors could benefit from new equipment technology as quickly as the domestic industry. Nevertheless, DARPA representatives and SEMATECH members showed little concern; their primary objective was to preserve the domestic equipment sector. Toward that end, it was important that domestic manufacturers maximize revenues and profits by selling abroad as well as in the United States.

At EPRI, one result of the deregulation of the electric power industry was the rise of nonregulated independent power producers, which competed aggressively for market share with EPRI's incumbent membership. The issue of whether to admit IPPs to consortium membership became a matter of extensive study and board discussion. The matter was decided in the affirmative, based fundamentally on a determination that EPRI's mission is to serve the broad electric power industry rather than electric utilities per se. At the same time, excluding IPPs could do little to affect intraindustry competition, since technology developed at EPRI would be readily accessible to the IPPs through the electric power industry's supply infrastructure.

In Bellcore's case, limiting membership to the seven RBOCs was undoubtedly done not so much for competitive reasons, since its nonmember clients included such important customers (and competitors) as GTE, Cincinnati Bell, Southern New England Telephone, and the local telephone companies belonging to GTE and Sprint. Membership restrictions trace back instead to the fact that Bellcore was formed to provide R&D services to the seven Baby Bells following their divesture from AT&T, and the loss of Bell Labs as a technology resource. Continuing to restrict membership to the RBOCs served simply to keep Bellcore's governance in the Baby Bells' hands, without cutting off revenues from external clients.

In sum, exclusionary practices arise out of a concern for competitive advantage. In formulating membership policies, then, it is useful to ask what the consortium's mission is and how it would tend to define the membership constituency. Would it be competitively advantageous to limit membership? If so, would such a policy be effective in restricting technology diffusion? And finally, what could other member subsets contribute to the consortium's mission in return for what they might receive?

Cohesiveness

Consortia governance is greatly facilitated by a cohesive membership constituency with a high commonality of interest in the consortium's R&D agenda. This is a given in single-task, limited-duration consortia; members are brought together because they share a common interest in pursuing some particular technological objective. Membership cohesiveness is more critical in the formation of *ongoing* collaborative enterprises. In consortia with broad and evolving agendas, there seems to be a certain inevitability in the divergence of interests and priorities within membership constituencies over time. But the existence of membership cohesiveness at the outset, based on a commonality of R&D interests, gives the consortium at least a good chance of coping with diverging member priorities as technical, competitive, and market environments change.

One factor that may influence the degree of diversity that can be tolerated among membership groups is the scope of the intended R&D agenda. The broader the agenda, as at EPRI or GRI, the closer the membership must cohere in its willingness to support a full array of R&D initiatives. Conversely, the narrower the scope, the more diverse the membership may be. If a consortium has a single purpose, as for example at SRC, a broad range of firms may share that one interest but diverge in other respects.

Vertical versus Horizontal Structure

Membership cohesiveness is at issue as well in whether a consortium's membership is to be structured vertically or horizontally. Vertically structured consortia are not unusual for single-task, limited-duration initiatives in which the collaborative objective and the allocation of funding are negotiated at the outset. In ongoing consortia with vertically structured membership, however, issues of R&D priorities and funding allocation often require constant renegotiation. GRI, for example, is vertically structured, with a membership that represents all segments of the gas industry: producers, transporters, and distributors. Accordingly, it has had to work through some difficult conflicts over how the funding burden should be divided among its three membership subsets. In vertically structured consortia, such conflicts are a manifestation of the natural contention that exists within any industry, as to how costs are to be assumed and profits taken at different levels of the value chain. Consortia that are so structured would seem to invite such contention, especially if a good deal of ambiguity exists, as in GRI's case, about how much each membership constituency actually pays.

The Free-rider Factor

A consortium's silent constituency are its free riders—the firms that benefit from its R&D output but do not have membership status and pay no fees. EPRI, for example, does not count among its members the more than two thousand small electric utilities in the United States. Like EPRI's membership, this constituency benefits from consortium R&D in domains such as environmental health and safety and the development of electric-powered end-products and improved power-generating technology. Much of these benefits filter through the suppliers EPRI engages to develop and commercialize new products and services.

At SRC, the free-rider phenomenon raises the specter that the consortium's current members may find little to justify continued dues payment. All the reports, papers, and documents that emanate from SRC-funded projects become immediately available through libraries and journals; and members and nonmembers have equal access to graduate students funded by SRC grants. In fact, as a 501(c)(6) (nonprofit) research organization, SRC is obligated by law to make the results quickly available to the public at large.[2] In recent years IRS auditors have probed the extent to which SRC has complied with this requirement. SRC's directors and management, then, may well ask whether their members will be willing to pay dues in support of SRC's research program if nonmembers have equal access to SRC outputs. But, if no firms were willing to pay to belong, the consortium would cease to exist, and all would be deprived of its benefits.

Several considerations are relevant to this issue. First, some elements of a consortium's product line are less expropriable than others. At EPRI, for example, such services as EPRINET (an online technical resource), the use of demonstration and test facilities, and technical and management consultation are benefits available only to the membership. At SRC, members gain from their involvement in the work of academic research teams and from computerized information on leading-edge research and those who produce it. In addition, there is lead-time value to the services provided to members.

Second, while the consortium's work may benefit free riders, members are likely to benefit at least proportionally, if not more so, from industry growth and development. That is, even though nonpayers gain, the returns to the fee-paying members may meet or exceed expected returns.

Finally, all six consortia discussed in this book were conceived in part to serve the national interest at an industry level—a condition of gaining government support that lends greater legitimacy to the undertaking. Thus, free-riding may be a burden that should be assumed, even at some indirect cost to the membership, in the interest of maintaining the support of government and other external constituencies.

The main point, however, is that while nonmembers may not be precluded from access to new technology, not all consortium products are available to nonmembers. And for those that are, the lead-time advantage members enjoy may have value. These considerations should more than justify the cost of membership if a consortium is to remain viable.

R & D S O U R C I N G S T R A T E G Y

There are essentially three options in consortia R&D sourcing modes. Consortia such as Bellcore and MCC rely on their internal technology staffs. SEMATECH, EPRI, SRC, and GRI use external contractors— mostly vendors who may turn the results of their R&D into commercial products and services. USCAR, a consortium formed by General Motors, Ford, and Chrysler, uses its member companies' technical staffs to carry out its projects similar to the way scientific development is often conducted in R&D joint ventures. A consortium may use one of these three modes as its primary sourcing strategy, and others as supplemental sourcing modes for particular projects. Thus while MCC's R&D is largely the responsibility of its internal staff, for some initiatives it may also draw on member-company suppliers. Bellcore, with its large internal staff, also relies extensively on private partners, Bellcore members, and others for specific projects.

Among the six consortia discussed in this book, the choice of a sourcing strategy is influenced by the nature of the consortium's mission, the inclinations of the founding CEO, and relevant precedent. SEMATECH, SRC, and EPRI have depended on external sourcing because their missions have included supply-industry infrastructure development. In the case of SRC, the relevant supply industry is the academic community, which does basic research in semiconductor design and manufacture. Bellcore, on the other hand, has as its mission the advance of operations technology for the seven RBOCs. Precluded by court decree from infrastructure development in telecommunications equipment manufacturing, Bellcore built up an internal staff of technologists both to carry out projects for its client-owners and to work with their research departments.

For both MCC and EPRI, the choice of an external R&D sourcing mode was influenced by the CEO's preferences. At MCC, Bobby Inman gave up trying to attract qualified technical talent from member companies, and quickly recruited a staff of full-time direct hires from outside. And while Joseph Swidler, the Federal Power Commission chair who first put forth the idea of a research institute for the electric power industry, would have preferred a buildup of internal R&D sourcing staff at EPRI, Chauncey Starr, EPRI's first CEO, chose otherwise. Starr thought the time and the extensive funding needed to build up an internal R&D capability would test the patience and willingness of EPRI's membership to support such an initiative. Instead, the buildup took place in program management. As of 1995, EPRI had a program management staff of almost three hundred. They administered more than two thousand active projects and a total of over three thousand research agreements with R&D contractors.

Precedent thought to be relevant also played a role. Bellcore was modeled after AT&T's Bell Labs, with its vast internal technology development resources; GRI was modeled after EPRI.

While R&D sourcing strategy may be dictated at first by a consortium's mission, once made, the choice of a sourcing mode tends to shape a consortium's subsequent direction. Those with large internal R&D staffs as a key resource—MCC and Bellcore, in particular—have gravitated toward becoming R&D contractors, soliciting and taking on projects for individual clients or client groups. Those with external R&D sourcing strategies have remained largely focused on infrastructure development, and have striven to maintain a common R&D agenda to serve the broad interests of their membership.

The relative merits of one or the other of these two R&D sourcing strategies are suggested, in part, in the foregoing discussion. External sourcing may be effective in infrastructure development insofar as it funnels resources into technology development at the supply-industry level. It also has the virtue of flexibility. An external sourcing network may be built up comparatively rapidly, and downsized with less dislocation and trauma than an internal staff. The profile of the external R&D resource network can also be readily transformed to accommodate changing research priorities. And the use of commercializing vendors as R&D contractors facilitates the diffusion of new technology to member companies and end-product markets. The other side of that coin, however, is that the use of such channels expedites technology diffusion to competitors and other nonmembers as well—that is, to free riders.

The advantages and disadvantages of internal R&D sourcing are just the reverse. Internal resources may be costly and time consuming to establish, and less flexible in adapting to shifts in R&D priorities or the need to downsize. At the same time, to the extent that internal R&D resources are focused on developing and transferring new technology to member companies, the ability to protect and control the use of new intellectual property may be somewhat greater than it is with external R&D sourcing systems.

Similarly, relying on member-company technical talent, the third R&D sourcing option, will allow better control over intellectual property, or at least delay its dissemination outside the consortium. This mode of sourcing is in effect a pooling of the complementary technology re-sources—personnel and laboratories—of member companies. It probably works best among companies of comparable size, with complementary R&D skills, as at USCAR.

PRODUCT-LINE STRATEGY

R&D consortia may define product-line strategy along four dimensions: (1) R&D domains (technology areas); (2) time horizons (short term versus long term); (3) product form (e.g., member-company problem solution, new end products, technology training for member-company employees); and (4) product options (bundled, unbundled, or customized).

R&D Domains

The consortium's technology domains are a function of its mission. At one extreme, a consortium may be formed to carry out one specific task; an example would be the CAD Framework Initiative, established to develop interoperability standards for computer-aided design. Another example would be the ARPA-initiated Microelectronics Manufacturing Science and Technology (MMST) program, dedicated to developing process sensors and a comprehensive computer-integrated manufacturing program, to enable real-time process control in semiconductor manufacturing plants.

At the other end of the scale, a mission may encompass the full range of technologies relevant to a membership constituency, as is the case at

EPRI, GRI, SRC, or Bellcore. In these environments, new science domains may move onto the consortium's R&D screen and others phase out
with the advance of technology and changing member priorities. The
choice of technology fields and the relative emphasis given to each then
becomes the concern of the consortium's board of directors and its senior
technical advisory committee. Thus, mission definition and evolving member priorities together drive the choice of R&D domains in which the
consortium will operate.

The Short-Term and Long-Term Choice

The choice between the long-term—say, five to ten years—and the short-
term—one to three years—time horizons seems now to pose only an
academic issue. Consortium members are generally unwilling to fund
work of a long-term and commensurately high-risk nature. Further, the
consensual decision-making processes that shape the R&D agenda are
likely to favor short-term, low-risk ventures. One exception is SRC, which
was formed to support the development of the academic infrastructure
focused on semiconductor design and manufacture. SRC funds research
that by its nature may be described as exploratory, of moderate to high
risk, and long term. SRC's time horizon, then, is congruent with that of
the academic world it supports. Thus SRC membership fees help to assure
the viability of a scientific resource essential to the long-term development
and competitive survival of the semiconductor industry.

Another exception to the foregoing statement are some consortia formed
with substantial government funding to contribute to U.S. industrial development. The statement of purpose for the Advanced Technology Program
(ATP) of the National Institute of Standards and Technology (NIST), for
example, reads in part as follows:

> The Advanced Technology Program works with U.S. industry to advance the
> nation's competitiveness—and economy—by helping to fund the development
> of high-risk but powerful new technologies that enable a broad spectrum of
> potential new applications, commercial products, and services. Through coopera-
> tive agreements with individual companies or groups of companies, large and
> small, the ATP invests in industrial projects to develop technologies with high-
> payoff potential for the nation.[3]

On its own, however, U.S. industry has shown a reluctance to support
long-term, high-risk research through consortia arrangements. As Admiral
Bobby Ray Inman observed in 1987:

What has happened over time is that there are more short-term expectations. . . . The high level executives who first organized MCC were looking at the mountains, but MCC is now being directed by people at the member companies who are looking at what is going to make their profit centers profitable.[4]

Similarly, Dr. Craig Fields, MCC's president from 1991 to 1994, noted: "MCC is engaged in more long-term projects than any other consortium, but that portion of the work is hard to sustain. The pressure from member companies is to shift the balance toward the short-term, as they are doing in their own internal R&D programs."[5] Thus, the desire for reduced-risk and near-term returns for consortia membership seems to have tilted consortia R&D agendas toward short-term (two- to three-year) projects. SRC is a special case in this respect.

Product Form

R&D consortia may deliver a variety of products. Among these are operational technology for member-company application; personnel training; new end products for consumer use; supply-industry infrastructure development; new software and hardware for member-company use; and industry problem solutions, such as those related to environmental impact. Also among consortium products are the benefits of participation—that is, current information on technological advances, networking opportunities, and the psychic rewards of being involved in consortium governance.

Several observations may be made regarding the array of product forms in which technology may be delivered. First, product-line strategy will often depend for its success on meeting the needs not of the member company as a single client, but of many individuals in the member-company organization. Hence the need to segment the consortium's market, not so much in terms of member companies or member sets, but in terms of job-related interest sets. Thus plant managers, research technologists, product development personnel, engineers, marketers, and administrators may comprise broad market segments. Within these, some may be further differentiated, as has been done in EPRI, according to technological field of interest. Such segmentation is the beginning point in formulating a product-line strategy.

Second, packaging new technology in a variety of forms, to meet a range of member-company personnel needs, is an essential element of membership retention. To the extent that a consortium serves multiple clients within member companies, it broadens its base of support. Furthermore, the benefits of consortium services may be more easily demonstrated and measured by individual product form than as some overall bundle of product offerings.

As a practical matter, however, the breadth of the R&D product line may depend on funding for the development of effective delivery systems—for technology-transfer staff, test centers, conference facilities, technical-paper delivery channels, and interactive telecommunications media. For example, though both EPRI and GRI serve regulated energy industries, EPRI has committed significantly greater resources to the development of R&D delivery systems, and is able to deliver R&D effectively in a broader range of product forms than GRI.

Finally, in delivering R&D advances in a range of forms, consortia may reduce the extent to which the new technology becomes accessible to free riders. While R&D focused on infrastructure development may become easily available to members and nonmembers alike, other consortium services—EPRI's EPRINET system,[6] for example, or Bellcore's member seminars—are less vulnerable to expropriation. To the extent that consortium benefits may be realized only by belonging, building and holding a membership constituency becomes easier.

In sum, broad product lines and effective technology delivery systems may be the key to building and sustaining membership in ongoing R&D consortia. Both should be oriented toward meeting the selective product needs not of member *companies,* but of member-company technology personnel, segmented in terms of their job-related interests.

Bundled versus Customized R&D Programs

An R&D program may be tailored to individual member needs at three levels. Members may choose from among the consortium's bundle of product offerings those that meet their particular needs. Second, they may have the option of allocating their annual fees to particular R&D areas and forgoing participation in others. At a third level, members may opt to sponsor customized R&D projects of interest to other individual members or member groups, as in the elective portion of Bellcore's R&D program. Moving along this scale of options is to go from a common R&D program, designed to meet the broad needs of a general membership, to an individualized program that responds to the needs, priorities, and ability to pay of individual members.

A major issue that confronts the boards and managements of ongoing consortia is the extent to which their programs should be bundled or should offer choices in what members may purchase, by R&D area or by project. The trend is toward unbundling; for while consortia are formed initially to serve some technology objective members share, over time members tend to drift apart in their R&D needs. This tendency may be particularly true in deregulating industries—natural gas, electric power, and telecommunications—where increasing interfirm rivalry is leading to strategic differentiation and differences in R&D priorities. Another factor underlying the trend may be the rising costs of research, and a resulting desire to share R&D costs yet still secure some measure of competitive advantage. Finally, declining consortium revenues, as is the case with MCC, could create pressure to promote customized R&D projects as a way of enhancing consortium income.

Certainly, some degree of unbundling would seem essential to meeting different member needs in ongoing consortia. The balance to be struck is between assuring the integrity of the consortium's common mission and responding to demand for tailored projects—at some cost, perhaps, in R&D scale economies. The goals to be achieved are membership retention, sufficient funding to produce and deliver a range of marketable services, and success in fulfilling the consortium's fundamental mission, as defined by member companies. EPRI has moved from one common package of R&D benefits for all member companies to providing additional options. Its Tailored Collaboration (TC) program, introduced in 1990, allows members to fund customized projects up to an amount equal to 25 percent of their annual membership dues. EPRI will match those funds from its general revenues if the project is deemed to have broad applicability to EPRI's membership as a whole. The TC component of the R&D program now accounts for approximately a third of EPRI's budget.

In 1994 EPRI announced its Progressive Flexibility (PF) option, to take effect in 1995. PF permits member companies to reduce their annual membership dues by as much as 20 percent, and at the same time to allocate dues payments to some combination of fourteen different business units, such as Transmission, Power Systems Operations, Nuclear Power, and Electric Transportation. Each has a different minimum price tag, stipulated not in dollars but as percentages of total dues, calculated in accordance with each member's retail kwh revenues. A requirement, however, is that 30 percent of each member's payment will go to support two core programs: Vital Issues and Strategic R&D. The first is essentially environmental R&D; the second addresses the need for development of basic technology in support of advances in electric power production, delivery, and end use, and environmental health and safety. Unless they are contributing 100 percent of the dues payable in accordance with their retail kilowatt-hour revenues, members may participate in, and receive the products of, only those business units to which they have subscribed.

EPRI seems to have configured its program options in a way that preserves its mission integrity, enhances revenues, and meets the needs of its member companies. Mission integrity is assured by providing cofunding incentives for those Tailored Collaboration projects that have broad relevancy to EPRI's membership as a whole, and by the requirement that members who take advantage of the Progressive Flexibility option invest approximately a third of their dues payments in the core R&D program. As for revenue enhancement, in 1994 the TC program generated approximately $100 million of EPRI's $600 million in revenues. In 1995, 28 percent of EPRI's members continued to participate in the full range of the consortium's programs while 72 percent elected the PF dues reduction opportunity. In the meantime, the dues reduction option together with program selectively is likely to attract more members and thus offset a decline in revenue from the existing member cohort. In any case, both the TC and PF options represent a significant response to the growing demand for product options among EPRI's members.

A Summary Comment

Ultimately, competing in the market for technology services, R&D consortia will survive and grow if they provide value to members and other funders. That is, they must offer the best option for sharing the costs of advancing operational technology, building infrastructure, and developing markets for end products. The creation of economic value goes beyond scientific discovery; until new technology can be delivered to members in product forms that meet their needs, true economic value may not be realized. Thus a range of product options and effective technology delivery systems are the key to creating value for members and sustaining their support.

Options may be provided on three levels. The first is member choice among products and services, provided within the bounds of a common R&D program. A second-level option would be to allow members to choose selectively among broad program areas in allocating their membership fees. A third-level option would be the funding of customized research projects, either by individual members or by partners. EPRI's Progressive Flexibility program is an example of the second level; its Tailored Collaboration program illustrates the third. At MCC and Bellcore, the the primary option offered to member companies is customized research.

With respect to breadth of product line, the six consortia discussed in this book fill different technology market niches, and differ with respect to what they offer member companies. Their product-line strategies seem to be determined by the extent of interfirm rivalry among member companies. In instances in which a consortium serves industries with relatively low interfirm rivalry, e.g., the electric power and natural gas industries, R&D programs and the range of products offered tend to be relatively wide. In SEMATECH, MCC, or SRC, which serve the highly competitive semiconductor industry, the range of work is far more limited and confined to noncompetitive domains.

Second, breadth of product line is a function of a consortium's funding level. Consortia with the necessary resources may process technology advances in a variety of forms and deliver them through a range of channels. Thus EPRI, which has three times the revenue of GRI, offers members a more extensive range of products and services than GRI, delivered through multiple channels.

PRICING POLICIES

Consortia revenue streams may include some combination of one-time shareholder fees, annual fees based on member income, fixed fees levied by member class, and project-cost reimbursements. Other revenues may come from government funding, contract R&D for nonmember clients, royalties and license fees, and equity interests in spinoff ventures. Government funding and contract R&D are often significant sources of revenue; royalties, license fees, and equity income are not major income sources.

Shareholder fees are often contributed by the consortium's original members to provide capital and cover startup costs. Such fees may continue to be levied on new members as the cost of entry. At MCC, for example, the price of a share of stock, pegged initially at $150,000, rose to $1 million in 1985, then dropped back to $250,000. MCC's equity members have governance rights and may share in royalty income as well.

Unlike the equity owners of private corporations, a consortium's shareholders can hardly measure the worth of their investment in expected capital gains and/or dividends. Rather, they may perceive their shareholder fees as an investment in future R&D benefits, both for individual members and for the industry and/or member set as a whole. For the founders, the shareholder fee may symbolize a commitment to the consortium's mission. Governance privileges may or may not come with the payment of cost-of-entry fees.

At EPRI, GRI, SEMATECH, and SRC, the single greatest source of revenue is the *annual membership fee,* the fee charged each member based on some percentage of the member's revenues. At EPRI, as noted earlier, the membership fee is proportional to retail kilowatt-hours; at SEMATECH, the measure for chip producers is semiconductor revenues; for members that use chips as components, the measure is semiconductor purchases.

The annual fee schedule may also be structured by *member class.* At SRC, the twenty firms in the member group, all with sales in excess of $30 million, pay fees based on sales or purchases of semiconductors, with a minimum of $65,000 and a maximum of over $3 million in annual fees. SRC affiliates—all with less than $30 million in sales—pay $500 per million of related sales. An associates category accommodates other R&D consortia and government agencies. SRC undertakes specific work for those members on a contract basis.

Finally, fees may be levied to cover individual *project costs.* MCC and Bellcore revenues are derived largely from such assessments. As noted earlier, about 14 percent of EPRI's revenues come from member payment for customized R&D—funds that are matched from EPRI's general funds.

Several pricing principles are reflected in the schedules of charges levied for consortium services. One is *relative value.* Calculating annual membership fees as some percentage of member sales implicitly recognizes that consortium output is likely to be proportionally beneficial to members. To make an important distinction, however, consortium pricing is *not* based on *true-value* principles. If consortium members receive benefits calculated at three to four times their membership dues, as is often claimed, consortium products are thus priced at far less than true value. (In a nonprofit organization, the owners of which are the customers, it is not likely that members would tolerate true-value pricing.)

The pricing of individual projects is typically *cost-based,* with surcharges, if any, calculated as a percentage of overall project costs. Finally, the use of different fee schedules for different membership categories, such as members, affiliates, and associates, classified in accordance with revenue levels and profit or nonprofit status, is *price discrimination.* Such pricing is a way of generating incremental revenue by setting fees based on the presumed *ability to pay.*

Overall, consortium pricing reflects the principle of *fairness,* a value deeply embedded in the culture of collaborative ventures. Thus, fairness was the essential issue in the contention over GRI's surcharge formula, which established the amount that interstate pipelines paid to fund GRI's R&D program.[7] And if consortium pricing systems are to be perceived as fair, they must bear a close relationship to the relative value of the benefits members receive.

R&D DELIVERY SYSTEMS

New technology is generally made operational through a range of channels. Most consortia use several channels, with perhaps an emphasis on one, depending on the core mission. Delivery systems include:

- · member-company assignees transferring new technology back to their respective companies;
- · consortium technical staff members working with member-company research, engineering, and production personnel;
- · consortium test and demonstration sites;
- · external research contractors taking new products and services to market;
- · mass communications in the form of technical papers and conferences; and
- · member-company representatives participating in consortia task force R&D planning and monitoring activities.

Thus SRC relies largely on the dissemination of academic research papers to member companies and at conferences. The consortium also involves member-company representatives in planning, monitoring, and mentoring roles in the university research community. New technology generated at SEMATECH becomes operational both through member-company assignees and the marketing of technically advanced equipment by its R&D subcontractors. And EPRI uses all but the first of the above channels in bringing its R&D discoveries to fruition.

The choice of a delivery channel depends on the nature of the R&D product—for instance, on whether it is a new technology for member-company use, or new equipment and end products. It depends as well on the technology receptor environment, e.g., the size of the member-company population and where along the industry value chain the technology is to be delivered. The subject of technology transfer mechanisms is discussed at greater length in the next chapter.

INTEGRATED STRATEGIES

The elements of a consortium's strategy are essentially interdependent. For example, compare EPRI, SEMATECH, and Bellcore. EPRI operates on three market levels, the electric power generation sector, its supply industry, and its end markets. Its purposes are to advance operational technology, build infrastructure, grow the electric power share of the U.S. energy market, and cope with issues of environmental health and safety. EPRI's members have a common interest in pursuing a broad, industry-oriented R&D agenda. EPRI's reliance primarily on annual membership fees based on member retail kwh revenues is consistent with this membership profile and mission. At the same time, EPRI has adapted its product and price strategies to the increasing demand for customized projects, as well as to differences in member-company R&D priorities. The use of external R&D sourcing fits EPRI's focus on supply-industry infrastructure development and on end-product market growth. EPRI's extensive R&D delivery system is designed to disseminate a wide range of products to its very large membership.

In comparison, SEMATECH has a relatively small membership characterized by a high level of interfirm rivalry but a common interest in the health of the U.S. semiconductor manufacturing equipment industry. Its policy of exclusivity—only U.S. companies qualify for membership—reflects its national purpose. Like EPRI, SEMATECH relies on a dues structure based on member-company semiconductor revenues or purchases. Like EPRI, it sources R&D externally. But because of its small membership and highly focused R&D program, SEMATECH's R&D delivery system is simpler than EPRI's. It relies on member-company assignees for the transfer of technology from supply-sector R&D contractors to member-company manufacturing plants.

Bellcore, formed as a pooled-technology resource for its seven client-owners, has the most extensive internal R&D staff of any consortium. Operating initially within territorial bounds, the RBOCs are becoming intensively competitive, both among themselves and with other sectors of the telecommunications and entertainment industries. Accordingly, their common R&D agenda seems to have atrophied, and Bellcore's role has become more one of serving the needs of individual members and membership subsets. The fact that Bellcore's revenues are derived largely on a project-by-project basis is consistent with the kind of business in which it is engaged.

In sum, the long-run sustainability of any collaborative R&D enterprise depends on the formulation of an integrated strategy in pursuit of a mission and on continuing strategic adaption as member needs and priorities change.

CHAPTER 5

Technology Transfer as Marketing

Implicit in early conceptualizations of R&D consortia was the idea that the consortium would create new technology and the member companies would put it to use. But early experience demonstrated that such a construct of the transfer process served neither the consortium nor its members well. At MCC, Bobby Ray Inman, MCC's first CEO, commented, "Some companies get in and they aggressively pull the technology out. Other companies lean back and sip through a long straw."[1] And MCC researchers noted that technical communications with member companies often "fell into a black hole."

Other consortia experienced the same frustrations and communication gaps. Member-company dissatisfaction with the transfer process led to the recognition that in addition to creating technology, delivering technology was an important function of the consortium. Thus in 1979, early in his term as EPRI's second president, Floyd Culler redefined EPRI's mission as RD&D: research, development, and demonstration. Culler began to build dissemination systems, to help member companies put new technology to use and to create markets for new products and services.

At GRI, an emphasis on technology delivery came later. In the early 1990s, at the urging of the board of directors, GRI's management undertook a review of the consortium's organization and operations. The review was intended to strengthen communications with member companies, develop more effective ways of transferring new technology, and help GRI to become more market driven. GRI's mission as well became RD&D. As one GRI officer observed: "GRI has been an R&D organization that did technology transfer; now we have to become a technology transfer organization that does R&D. This is very significant in how we think and how we do our jobs. We have to change the organization; we have to change the processes." As Dr. Court Skinner, director of the Fairchild

Research Center of the National Semiconductor Corporation, pointed out, technology transfer is essentially a marketing process:

> The idea behind technology transfer is a product gets transferred from a laboratory into—say—somebody's production operation. But if I'm a professor at university X, I want all the member companies to use my research. That's technology broadcasting. What you would call that is "marketing," but "marketing" is not an acceptable term. So we confuse ourselves by calling it "technology transfer" and say all we have to do is take it from one laboratory to one production operation. We lump under technology transfer a lot of stuff that really has to do with communication: video conferencing, research papers, data base abstracts. While we can't call it marketing, that's what we're doing. We have to say "technology transfer" because that sounds right.[2]

A broad conception of the consortium's role in technology diffusion— that is, its role in marketing—developed at different points in the history of all six consortia discussed in this book. But it was never clearly articulated in their founding visions. Why not? One reason is probably that the idea of marketing technology often seems to run counter to the culture of research enterprises. At MCC during its honeymoon years under Inman, for example, the high quality of life was evident in the low rate of personnel turnover—only about 3 percent. MCC's culture changed during Dove's tenure, however. One reason was that MCC scientists were called on to spend increasing amounts of their time—up to half—on technology transfer. Personnel turnover increased.[3]

In some instances budget restrictions imposed by regulatory agencies or member companies precluded expenditures for so-called marketing activities. GRI is a case in point. Guidelines imposed on GRI by the Federal Power Commission ruled out spending on "consumer surveys, advertising, promotions, or items of like nature." Bellcore established a Client Relations department in 1987 in recognition of the need to better manage its business relationship with owner-clients and to better market Bellcore products to outside customers. The organization included seven client account teams plus a thirty-person direct salesforce serving non-member customers. In 1991, however, Bellcore's owner-clients expressed concern about the cost-effectiveness of funding the group's $4 million to $5 million budget. While Heilmeier, Bellcore's new CEO, believed that the group's activities were important in carrying out Bellcore's mission, the directors strongly urged that it be downsized.

Perhaps the major reason for the low priority given these functions in the past is that technology diffusion is inherently difficult. Often, those who can benefit from a new technology and are qualified to put it to use are difficult to identify and reach. Furthermore, technology diffusion, like marketing in private corporations, is often costly to support. And finally, efforts to put new technology to use often set in motion countervailing forces of resistance.

With the rapid pace of technical innovation and more than two decades of experience, however, the requirements of effective *technology diffusion* are now better understood. Technology *transfer*, perceived in the early years as a one-way street between two points, the point of origin and the point of use, was thought to be largely the responsibility of the user. In contrast, current ideas of technology *diffusion* recognize the following:

- Technology diffusion calls for an understanding of the needs of different market segments.
- Reaching markets for new technology at the member level and beyond requires a variety of tools and techniques.
- Along with the recognition of technology diffusion as the consortium's primary responsibility comes the need for different measures of consortium performance.

Experience has shown that the requirements of technology diffusion vary significantly from one consortium to another—the differences being no less significant than those that distinguish Coca-Cola from Dow Chemical. Differences reflect the nature of the consortium's mission, the size and composition of its membership group, and the type of product line. Compare, for example, SEMATECH and EPRI. At SEMATECH, the great majority of researchers are member-company assignees. Residing at the consortium's facilities in Austin, Texas, for periods of one to four years, they are the vertical links between about 130 domestic tool suppliers and major U.S. semiconductor manufacturers. As members of SEMA-TECH project teams, they work with equipment suppliers to define the requirements for next-generation equipment for semiconductor fabrication plants and to develop technologies to meet those needs. As members of technology teams in their own companies, they help to plan for the incorporation of new technical advances, both in updating old plants and designing new ones. Finally, they transmit the performance requirements for successive generations of semiconductor manufacturing equipment to suppliers, working with them to develop the new technologies and helping them to implement advances in the factories of the future.

At EPRI, the technology delivery process is multifaceted. It includes programs for working with the consortium's more than seven hundred members to determine their needs for new technology, and then for helping them to implement new technological developments in advanced power generation and distribution systems. At the membership level, new project ideas emanate largely from task forces and program and project committees, on which the member companies are represented. EPRI's program managers and project integrators are responsible for carrying out such work through selected research contractors. Technology Transfer Managers (TTMs), who work with program managers, play a key role in putting new technology into practice in member firms. Member Relations Executives (MREs), located in EPRI's seven regional field offices, are the bridge between TTMs and designated Managers of EPRI Technology Transfer (METTs) in member utilities.

Putting new advances into practice requires EPRI to identify those utilities—and in particular, those persons—for whom the technology fills a need. Toward that end, EPRI has developed the Technical Interest Profile (TIP). Completed by personnel at all levels in member utilities, it serves to identify the target audiences for any of a wide range of technology applications. For example, the list includes distribution instrumentation and control, electric transportation, generation maintenance practices, and nuclear corrosion control. One-page bulletins on new developments are disseminated to those who have an interest in relevant technologies, and complete reports are sent out on request. EPRI conducts over two hundred workshops each year to communicate new technical developments to member-company representatives in interactive sessions. To make EPRI's technical knowledge as available as possible to member utility operators, the Institute developed EPRI-NET, a computerized E-mail network through which utility personnel may access EPRI documents and confer directly with EPRI project managers.

In the early technology adoption phase, one or more host utilities are asked, or volunteer, to implement a technical advance and serve as demonstration sites. Successful implementation is then widely publicized through technical papers and bulletins. In addition to documenting innovations, the bulletins recognize those individuals in host utilities and at EPRI who have played key roles in their creation and implementation. EPRI's president sends personal letters of commendation to those who are credited with breakthroughs, both at EPRI and in host utilities.

Plaques are also presented at award ceremonies held at the consortium's headquarters and at host utility sites.

The major vehicle for disseminating new products for utilities and consumer and industrial markets are the commercializing partners with whom EPRI contracts for R&D work. After developing new products, these partners then take them to market. To achieve broad market exposure, EPRI sometimes works to build the base of new suppliers. For example, after the development of a microwave clothes dryer, the project manager made a videotape showing the new dryer in operation and explaining its advantages. The tape was shown to appliance manufacturers to stimulate their interest in adding such an item to their product lines.

In brief, at EPRI, technology delivery is marketing. It relies on member-company participation on task forces and advisory committees for marketing research information on member needs. At the member-company level, its market segmentation scheme as delineated in the Technical Interest Profile is structured largely in accordance with job-related R&D interests. To identify potential technology users, the consortium relies on direct-mail announcements of new developments targeted at member-company personnel in relevant TIP categories. EPRI also fields a direct salesforce called the Member Relations Executives (MREs) in the seven regional offices to identify and communicate with qualified decision makers and technology implementers through designated METTs in member companies. Both the EPRINET system and the consortium's field demonstration and test sites serve as customized communications vehicles, reaching a geographically dispersed membership constituency. In providing attractive opportunities to develop markets for new products and services to its commercializing R&D contractors, EPRI pursues a push marketing strategy. And in going directly to appliance manufacturers to stimulate interest in a new product, EPRI uses pull marketing techniques.

Throughout, stress on creating buyer motivation, both personal and economic, is central to EPRI's marketing strategy. Personal recognition and the promise of enhanced operational efficiencies create incentives for individuals and managers to take the initiative—and the risk—of introducing new technology.

SIMPLE TECHNOLOGY DIFFUSION SYSTEMS

For purposes of this discussion, technology diffusion systems may be classified as *simple* or *complex*. Simple systems rely primarily on personal communications links with limited numbers of members. Complex systems are comprised of multiple channels to a large membership base, including personal communications, print and electronic media, the industry supply and market infrastructures, and the consortium's R&D planning structure.

The essential challenges for consortia such as SEMATECH, MCC, SRC, and Bellcore lie in identifying qualified receptors of new technology in member companies, in securing their commitment and motivation, and in assuring the effective transmittal of new technology.

Difficulty in identifying qualified receptors varies from one consortium to another. At SEMATECH, where the great majority of technical personnel are on assignment from member companies, the receptors are typically part of the assignee's home-company network and/or the engineering team of which the assignee is a member. Herein lies the great advantage of staffing consortia with assignees in a simple-diffusion environment. According to William Spencer, SEMATECH's CEO:

> The most satisfied members of SEMATECH are those that have an internal support structure for capitalizing on SEMATECH programs. One of our key companies feels that the internal mechanism is at least 60% as large as their annual investment in SEMATECH. Just as champions were essential for getting SEMATECH off the ground, champions in each member company are essential for getting the insertion of program results. Today, there is a program manager at SEMATECH and a program champion for each key program. Those two individuals are responsible for determining customer requirements for each member company and determining the return on investment to that member company.[4]

Figure 5.1 summarizes the relationships among members of SEMATECH's simple diffusion system.

At MCC, staffed largely with direct hires, receptor identification is more difficult. Initially, MCC sought simply to transfer technology as "standard technology packages," but according to MCC researchers, the "technology just seemed to lay there." In time, this vehicle was supplemented by technical and research reports, shareholder briefings, videotapes, workshops, and video conferencing.[5] Success seemed to depend on the emergence of member-company product champions. One example was the Proteus project.[6] In mid-1987 MCC proudly announced that Proteus, a technology developed in the consortium's Advanced Computer Architecture Research Program, would be commercialized by NCR. Proteus was an expert-system development environment, or software system "shell," that could be loaded with detailed knowledge about a specific problem. NCR engineers had used the Proteus shell to develop an expert system for advising designers of integrated circuits. They found it emulated the

Figure 5.1 SEMATECH: A Simple Technology Diffusion System

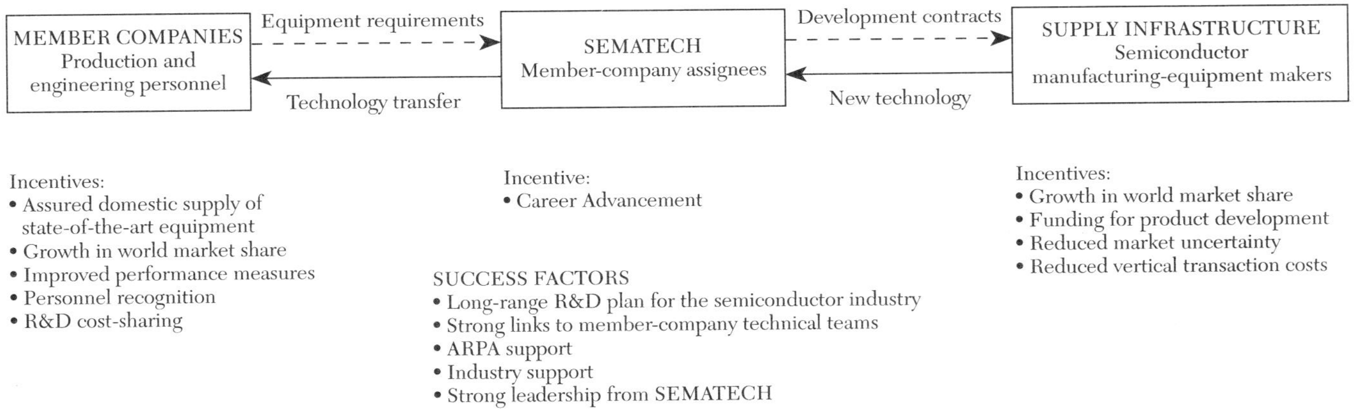

MEMBER COMPANIES
Production and engineering personnel

Equipment requirements - - - - - →

Technology transfer

SEMATECH
Member-company assignees

Development contracts - - - - →

New technology

SUPPLY INFRASTRUCTURE
Semiconductor manufacturing-equipment makers

Incentives:
• Assured domestic supply of state-of-the-art equipment
• Growth in world market share
• Improved performance measures
• Personnel recognition
• R&D cost-sharing

Incentive:
• Career Advancement

SUCCESS FACTORS
• Long-range R&D plan for the semiconductor industry
• Strong links to member-company technical teams
• ARPA support
• Industry support
• Strong leadership from SEMATECH

Incentives:
• Growth in world market share
• Funding for product development
• Reduced market uncertainty
• Reduced vertical transaction costs

expert knowledge that results from years of human experience in designing microcircuits. Installed at engineering work stations, the product would review proposed circuit designs and offer advice on how to improve them.

Robin Steele was a highly motivated young NCR engineer with a clear concept of how Proteus could be incorporated into a specific product she was working on. She went to Austin, interacted with MCC researchers, "grabbed hold of the technology and dragged it out." As a result, MCC researchers got timely, useful feedback from Steele on the functions they were building into Proteus.

In July, MCC and NCR held a press conference at the Hayden Planetarium, at which presentations were made by high-level people including Malcolm Baldrige, then secretary of commerce. Steele received an award from NCR's president. She was surprised at the attention given her. "I really had no idea that the product and the synergism between MCC and NCR would be such a hot topic. It really did more for my career than I ever expected."

This example suggests that technology transfer is most effective when it is (1) carried out by highly motivated individuals on the receiving end, (2) internally supported by top management, (3) executed in close proximity with consortium scientists, and (4) performed in a rewards-based atmosphere. The effectiveness of technology transfer depends critically on how relevant the new technology is to the receptor's work and his or her time horizon. Speaking of technical personnel who worked as mentors of SRC-funded university researchers, Dr. Pallab Chatterjee, president of personal productivity products at Texas Instruments, noted:

> Those whose responsibility in TI is to do industrial research, as opposed to development, have done better in the mentoring relationship with universities; the technology gets transferred in through regular internal research channels. The product development people don't do so well in the university relationship because there is an expectation gap. The mentor demands that the universities do things that are beyond their capability. More and more, we are realizing that it is better for the SRC members to bring the technology in through the research side rather than through product development. Another thing has to do with the time horizon that we ask the university professor to take. The closer in to the product world, the closer in you would like the professor to be, but that isn't what they are set up to do. The effectiveness of the mentoring process depends on the willingness of the mentor to value the work that he is mentoring, and that can depend largely on his job focus.[7]

Daniel Fleming of IBM added, "I try very hard to get a match between the people who have the right job assignment and can make use of the information once it's known. If they don't have the right job assignment, then they are still pushing it inside the corporation instead of pulling it in."[8]

While much technology transfer may take place through relatively passive media, such as research papers and conferencing, at some point it often involves direct, interactive communication between member-company receptors and consortium transmitters. To be effective, such communication requires transmitter-receptor *proximity.*[9] Further, the technology transmittal process is facilitated by utilizing well-established and well-maintained channels. The process goes more easily at SEMATECH because technology transfer is ongoing, with member companies continually assimilating new technical advances in semiconductor plant design and operation. Transfer to a changing constituency involved in one-time projects would be more difficult, for lack of established transmittal channels.

Clearly, proximity facilitates the process of adapting new technology and tailoring it to the receptor's needs. Further, the personalization of the process may help to reassure member-company receptors of the quality of the new technology, and reduce the perceived risks of making it operational. At SRC, proximity is perceived as a critical element in the transfer of new knowledge from university laboratories to member-company representatives. Dr. James Freedman, SRC's vice president for research integration, noted:

> Some companies are in close proximity to many of the universities which we fund. But for many, the costs of traveling to research sites can be quite prohibitive. As a consequence, we have been working to reduce the travel expense barrier. We've created what we call virtual meetings, using electronic communication to get people together in a way that simulates face-to-face meetings. We lease satellite communication facilities and put on full-day seminars. These are real-time television programs where we bring in speakers on special topics and where anybody who has a microwave link can be beamed up and down to whoever subscribes through a microwave dish. We select the time period so that it is early morning on the West Coast and runs until early evening on the East Coast, that is from about 11:00 until 2:00 or 3:00, a four-hour time period.
>
> We've also brought in a PictureTel, which is a video telephone hookup. This is great for one-on-one and is being put to use in mentoring meetings. Many of our companies have these systems installed but many of the universities do not. This past year we funded PictureTel installations at two universities, Carnegie-Mellon in Pittsburgh and Stanford in Palo Alto, for use in mentoring and for tech transfer seminars at which researchers report on their work. It's a good system for point-to-point connections, and we have had several very successful East Coast–West Coast workshop meetings with 4–5 people in each room. We

can do real-time problem solving because the PictureTel capability includes video cameras for projecting graphics and images.[10]

COMPLEX TECHNOLOGY DIFFUSION SYSTEMS

As has been noted, among the conditions that make technology diffusion a complex process is a very large membership base, with multiple potential receptors. A second condition that adds to the complexity of the diffusion process is the fact that consortia work in multiple technology application environments. At both GRI and EPRI, new technology is used (1) to advance member-company practice in areas such as energy production and distribution and environmental health and safety; (2) to contribute to the growth of end-product markets; and (3) to develop the utility industry's supply infrastructure.

At the Membership Level

As noted, success in technology diffusion at the membership level depends on having systems in place for identifying and serving potential receptors through "user-friendly" channels. It also depends on motivating qualified receptors to undertake the introduction of new technology in their work environments. A key factor in motivating technology implementers is optimizing the risk/reward equation. EPRI minimizes risk by setting up showcase demonstrations of new technology at one or more host utilities and cofunding the installation costs. The startup investment is thus reduced by half for early adopters, and later adopters are assured of success. Successes are also publicized to the membership at large through bulletins. EPRI's network of forty-four test facilities also serve to reduce the risk of implementing new technology. Some of these are dedicated to the advance of technology in power generation, transmission, and distribution, such as the EHV Cable test laboratory, the Underground Cable test facility, and the High Sulphur test center. Others are user-industry oriented, such as the centers for mining, food processing, textiles, and foundry.

Rewards come in the form of improved departmental performance measures, as well as individual recognition for those at EPRI and the host utility who may be directly involved with the innovation. Individual recognition comes through articles in EPRI bulletins, letters of commendation from top managers in member companies, and awards ceremonies. EPRI managers take the initiative to ensure that pioneering work is made visible at the host utility and throughout the electric power industry.

The objectives are both to reward current technical achievement and to encourage future risk-taking.

At the Supply and Market Infrastructure Levels

The diffusion of new technology through supply infrastructures and end-product markets requires collaboration with commercializing firms, first on the development of new technologies and then on their introduction to the marketplace in the form of new products and services for member companies and/or their customers. Qualified vendors must be recruited and offered attractive profit-generating opportunities. Often, selecting commercializing partners comes down to assessing their capabilities for successful product/market introductions, and their incentives or disincentives for doing so. Thus a leading supplier with a well-developed product line and distribution channel might be an ideal candidate to take a new product to market—except that the product might threaten to cannibalize sales of some existing items in the supplier's line. If so, a strong disincentive to aggressive market development exists. Small firms with no conflicting commitments may make better commercializing partners. Or the consortium program manager may conclude that as a practical matter, there is little choice, and the consortium must team up with the end-product market leaders in both the product development and commercialization phases.

Successful product development may depend as well on forming collaborative ventures with commercializing partners, member companies, and sometimes public agencies. The wind-power alliance formed under EPRI's aegis is a case in point. In spite of strong government support through R&D funding and tax credits in the 1970s and early 1980s, wind power failed to become an economical energy source. Only after U.S. Windpower (USW), the leading manufacturer of electric turbines, designed a variable-speed unit with improved reliability and operational efficiency did the time seem right to EPRI program managers to move wind-power development forward.

A memorandum written by an EPRI program manager in 1986 noted the apparent lack of interest in wind power on the part of the utilities, probably due to their prior experience with wind turbines as an unreliable and more costly electric power source than conventional generating plants. The memorandum stated in part:

> What is missing for utilities is a sense of ownership of the smaller wind turbine technology. I believe any success-oriented program for utility-grade wind power technology development must provide this sense of ownership as a key ingredient.

An opportunity with potential for significantly advancing wind power technology has emerged from our recent workshop. If structured properly, it should also improve prospects for utility acceptance of wind power. The project concept is to assemble and then conduct a five to seven year development program for the next generation of wind turbine technology. This is envisioned as a several hundred kilowatt turbine employing 1990's solid-state-electronic variable speed technology, and designed as an integral system to take advantage of all of the positive features. . . that variable speed can offer.

We would need to involve a major wind turbine manufacturer who has a firm technology base and a commitment to technology advancement in the long term toward the utility bulk power market. And we would need to involve two or more utilities with sufficient interest to co-fund the effort. EPRI would offer the concept, the link between manufacturer and users, coordination and management, and some funding. The manufacturer would provide business concessions to the co-funding utilities and to EPRI, commensurate with funding contributions. A strong attempt should be made to involve at least one utility outside of California.

Following this line of reasoning, in 1990 EPRI formed a consortium of USW, Pacific Gas & Electric, and Niagara Mohawk. Its purpose was to advance variable-speed drive technology in order to increase its efficiency, lengthen machine life, and lower the cost of power. Under the terms of the arrangement, USW contributed $13 million toward the development of a variable-speed wind turbine, Pacific Gas & Electric and Niagara Mohawk $3 million each, and EPRI $1 million. USW would hold any patents related to the technology, and EPRI and the two other utilities would share in the royalties.

In the meantime, EPRI, with USW and the DOE, established wind-power advisory groups to build interest in installing turbines and inform utilities of the status of the technology. In addition, in 1991 the electric utilities and some federal and state agencies charted promising wind-power locations throughout the nation. EPRI's program leader and USW's president visited fifteen major utilities in states with promising high-wind areas—a campaign that was instrumental in developing the early market for the new machine.

By 1995, seventeen thousand wind turbines were in place, mostly in California, and were generating 3 billion kilowatt-hours per year. The power they produced displaced the equivalent of 5 million barrels of oil and avoided 1.3 million tons of carbon emissions. Energy costs from the machines were in the range of 7 to 10 cents per kilowatt-hour, which was marginally competitive, and some contracts were signed for less than 5 cents per kilowatt-hour. In the long run, 4 cents per kilowatt-hour was considered achievable, and 3 cents possible, compared with about 5 cents per kilowatt-hour for power produced in an efficient coal-burning facility. Of course, the value of wind power is diminished by the fact that it is operative only when the wind blows.

The wind-power alliance formed by EPRI became the vehicle for developing an end-product market for an alternative form of energy generation. By involving a range of interested parties and industry influencers, and by creating a sense of industry ownership, EPRI secured the commitment and involvement essential to implementing a new technology.

Figure 5.2 diagrams EPRI's complex system for technology diffusion.

S U M M A R Y

Perceptions of the requirements of effective technology dissemination have evolved considerably since the six consortia studied in this book were founded. Then, technology diffusion was perceived essentially as a one-way street, with the consortium creating new technology and its members taking it away. The vehicles for the transfer of technology were technical reports, conference briefings, and member-company liaisons. But consortium members quickly became dissatisfied with the failure to move technical advances promptly into practice, and pressed consortia managements to take greater responsibility for their diffusion and be more "market oriented."

What explains the initial reluctance on the part of consortia to be more proactive in the diffusion of technology? Probably the idea of having to *sell* technology seemed alien to those engaged in scientific discovery. In this respect, it may be observed that consortia that conducted their R&D internally—MCC for one—had more difficulty in adapting culturally to the idea of marketing technology than others—EPRI, for example—that carried out R&D using external resources. In some consortia, members and regulatory commissions were initially unwilling to support an organizational investment in diffusion functions, preferring to concentrate their funding on the creation of technology. Finally, the diffusion of technology is inherently difficult; in essence, it is the marketing of change, often in the face of countervailing resistance.

Currently, consortia managements recognize that R&D deliverables consist not only of new technology per se but of member-company problem-solving, employee training, the dissemination of technical information, networking opportunities, and indeed the psychic rewards of belonging. Dissemination programs must be tailored to the interests of multiple

Figure 5.2 EPRI: A Complex Technology Diffusion System

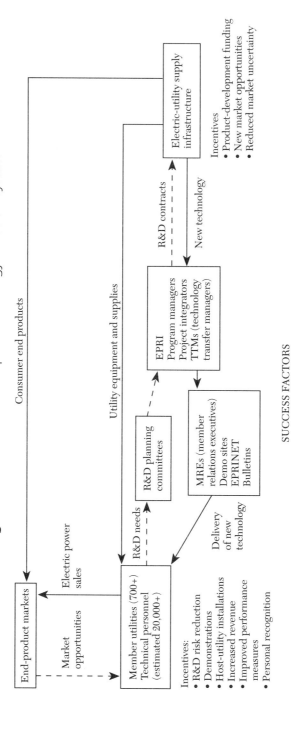

segments within member companies and among external constituencies, each of which has different needs, may perceive the consortium's product differently, and may need to be reached through different communications vehicles.

The requirements of effective technology diffusion vary considerably from one type of consortium to another. Thus diffusion functions at SEMA-TECH are markedly different from those at EPRI. At SEMATECH, member-company assignees are the primary means for developing and then transferring technical advances from the suppliers of semiconductor manufacturing equipment to their customers, the major U.S. semiconductor manufacturers. In a simple diffusion system such as this, effective transfer depends on (1) identifying qualified technology receptors in member companies; (2) establishing and maintaining ongoing communications channels; (3) providing for frequent contact between technology transmitters and receptors; (4) putting in place reward systems to assure recognition for the creative contributions of both receptors and transmitters; and (5) assuring top management's support. The great benefit of having member-company assignees as transmittal agents is their access to internal technology implementation networks. Thus SEMATECH's experience suggests that success in technology transmittal depends heavily on member companies' building and maintaining effective systems not only for receiving new technical advances but for generating technology requirements as well.

At EPRI technology diffusion is more complex, for two reasons. First, EPRI has a membership base of over seven hundred utilities, each of which may have hundreds of potential clients, or technology receptors. Second, in addition to advancing member-company technology and working to build the industry's supply infrastructure, EPRI also has extensive programs for end-product market development. Dissemination of technology at the membership level requires systems for identifying and responding to client needs—that is, user-friendly interactive channels. EPRI's TIP system serves as a client self-identification mechanism; EPRI-NET, as an interactive communications channel.

Another element in technology diffusion involves minimizing the risks of adopting new technology and maximizing the rewards. EPRI addresses the risks by cofunding demonstration installations, maintaining test facilities for member-company use, and publicizing success stories. Rewards come on three levels: at the member-company level, in the form of attractive returns on technology investment and a public image as an innovator;

at the department level, in the form of improved performance measures; and to the individual, through awards and publicity within the firm and throughout the industry.

In building the supply infrastructure as well as end-product markets, the key to success is the selection of qualified commercializing partners. That may mean weighing the marketing capabilities of outside firms against potential disincentives, which may arise as products based on new technology conflict with or compete against established products. It may also mean selecting the right number of commercializing partners—more than one, to ensure some degree of competition, but not so many firms that the market opportunity is substantially diminished for each competitor.

End-product market development may require as well skill in forming vertical alliances among a limited number of member companies and commercializing partners. Drawn into such alliances by profit opportunities, if effectively managed, its members may well lead the industry in the adoption of new technical advances. A case in point is the alliance formed by EPRI to develop new wind-power technology as an economic source of energy, and to introduce it to the electric utility industry.

Over the last two decades, consortium members have increasingly demanded improved R&D delivery. Consortium performance is now being judged to a greater degree on the extent to which the consortium is successful in making new technology operational in the form of advanced processes, products, and technical education. Consortium managers and governing boards are coming to recognize that building and maintaining effective channels for the diffusion of technology may take substantial funding, as marketing does in private corporations. This is a significant change in thinking from the precept that the role of the consortium is to do research and development, and the role of members is to take it away.

CHAPTER 6

R&D Consortia in the United States, Japan, and Europe

In the world's three major industrialized areas—the United States, Japan, and Europe—R&D consortia emerged at different times, and have played different roles in their respective economies. This chapter focuses primarily on the rise of R&D consortia in the United States and its contribution to the advancement of technology in the context of the country's overall R&D sourcing systems. Descriptions of consortia in Japan and Europe follow, primarily for purposes of comparison.

R&D CONSORTIA IN THE UNITED STATES

The R&D consortium first appeared in the United States with the founding of the Electric Power Research Institute (EPRI) in 1973. The Gas Research Institute (GRI), modeled after EPRI, was incorporated in 1976 and began operating in 1978. Both were conceived as ongoing organizations to serve broad industry research and development needs; both were open to all members of their respective domestic industries.

What little collaborative research may have been done before 1973 came under the aegis of trade associations. The American Gas Association included an R&D component in its PAR (Promotion, Advertising, and Research) program, and devoted about $10 million annually to gas utility research. Another $10 million, cofunded to the extent of $20 million by government sources, went to research in coal gasification, a program that was taken over by GRI when it began operating in 1978.[1]

The first consortium to bring together competing companies in an unregulated industry was SRC, which was established in 1982. As noted earlier, its mission is to fund university research and the training of graduate students in silicon-based semiconductor design and manufacturing. SRC was a delicate experiment in competitors working together to develop what has come to be called *precompetitive* R&D. Other computer and semiconductor consortia followed: Microelectronics and Computer Technology Corporation (MCC) in 1982 and SEMATECH in 1987. At the end of 1995, 592 consortia were registered under the National Cooperative Research and Production Act of 1993 (originally the 1984 National Cooperative Research Act).

R&D Consortia: Why Now?

What are the conditions that have fostered the rise of R&D consortia in the United States over the last two decades? The following are relevant: national crises that have created the need for new technologies to cope with external threats; relatedly, the emergence of an industry-level R&D agenda; a legislative climate conducive to forming R&D alliances; escalating industrial research and development costs; changing perceptions of competitive technical advantage; and changing industry R&D sourcing patterns.

National Crises and Industry R&D Agendas. The founding of four of the six consortia in this study is directly connected to national crises. GRI was established largely because of a perceived shortage of natural gas and escalating oil prices resulting from the Arab oil embargo of 1973. Oil rose in price from $3 to $12 per barrel, raising national concern about the nation's heavy dependence on imported oil. Before that, a twelve-hour power blackout in the northeastern United States and eastern Canada (in November 1965) had raised widespread doubts about the reliability of the domestic electric power system. Concerns about the reliability of electric power and the preservation of safe and clean air, water, and land resources led to the passage of the National Environmental Protection Act (1969), setting the stage for the formation of the Electric Power Research Institute in 1973. For both EPRI and GRI, the result was strong governmental support of R&D consortia as vehicles for developing alternative energy sources, for finding ways to conserve existing supplies of oil and gas, for coping with environmental issues, and for assuring the reliability of energy production and delivery. Thus the high priority that

EPRI gave to research on coal gasification, and that GRI gave to processes for extracting methane from coal, addressed national needs.

The initiatives for starting SEMATECH and MCC can be traced directly to threats posed to the domestic semiconductor industry by the Japanese. In particular, the announcement in 1981 of the formation of ICOT (Japan's Fifth Generation Computer Project) triggered a sharp response in the United States among leaders in industry and the Department of Defense (DOD). At a meeting convened by William C. Norris, then CEO of Control Data, in Orlando, Florida, in February 1982, fifty senior-level executives from seventeen leading computer and semiconductor manufacturers talked of crisis. Jerry Sanders, CEO of Advanced Micro Devices, stated, "The only reason I'm here is because of the Japanese. They are competent and they will kill us if we don't do something. We must do something different in coordination." Charles Sporck, CEO of National Semiconductor, added: "Our lack of a U.S. industrial policy is our biggest problem. . . . Somehow the country has to be rallied to meet the cooperative effort here like MITI. We must focus on how to survive—it's overwhelming."[2] The outcome of the Orlando meeting was a decision to move ahead with an R&D consortium.

SEMATECH's founding, as well, is tied directly to the Japanese threat, made even more urgent by an IBM study that documented the alarming deterioration of the U.S. semiconductor manufacturing-equipment infrastructure. At the same time, the need for increased semiconductor research was made apparent by a Hewlett-Packard study in 1979, which showed conclusively that the quality of Japanese-made semiconductors was significantly higher than that of U.S.-made chips. HP compared the quality of semiconductors made by three U.S. vendors and three Japanese suppliers. On arrival, no Japanese chip failed inspection, while 50 to 100 of every 50,000 U.S.-produced semiconductors did. In use, the worst American chip was twenty-seven times more likely to fail than the best Japanese product. These results alarmed U.S. chip manufacturers when they were made public in 1980.[3] Thus external threats created an industry-government R&D agenda of considerable urgency, and forced collaboration on a level that might not otherwise have been feasible at this point in time in a nation strongly committed to the concepts of competition and a free market economy.

A Favorable Governmental Climate. It was not until the passage of the National Cooperative Research Act (NCRA) in 1984 that the way became clear for companies in a wide range of unregulated industries to join together in cooperative research ventures. The initiative for enacting the NCRA came out of the founding of Microelectronics and Computer Technology Corporation (MCC). In March 1982, one month after the Orlando meeting, the directors of the Electronics Industries Association proposed the legislation. William Norris, Admiral Bobby Ray Inman (MCC's first CEO), and Representatives Jake Pickle and Jim Wright of Texas, where MCC chose to locate, lobbied hard and successfully for its passage. Without the assurance that such collaborative arrangements did not violate antitrust law, it would have been difficult if not impossible to bring together in an R&D consortium rival firms like Digital Equipment, Honeywell, Control Data, NCR, RCA, Motorola, National Semiconductor, Advanced Micro Devices, Harris, and Sperry.

Under the NCRA, parties to R&D collaborations may limit their exposure to antitrust damages by filing a notification with the Department of Justice and the Federal Trade Commission. The NCRA states in part:

> The conduct of any person in making or performing under a contract to carry out a joint research and development venture shall not be deemed illegal *per se;* such conduct shall be judged on the basis of its responsibleness taking into account all relevant factors affecting competition including but not limited to, effects on competition in properly defined, relevant research and development markets.[4]

In a news release announcing the new legislation, then Assistant Attorney General J. Paul McGrath stated:

> On October 11, 1984, President Reagan signed into law S.1841, the National Cooperative Research Act of 1984 (P.L. 98-462). Cooperative research and development efforts may improve productivity, bring better products to consumers sooner and at lower cost, and enable American business and industry to keep pace with foreign competitors in a world increasingly dependent on technological innovation. By significantly improving the legal climate, the National Cooperative Research Act should stimulate innovative research and development by the private sector.[5]

Registration under the act is optional. Some consortia, such as EPRI and GRI, have not registered, partly because the industries they represent seem less vulnerable to the antitrust law and partly because of the paperwork involved; reregistration is required with each change in the membership roster.

Another favorable legislative initiative was the Omnibus Trade Bill of 1988, which specifically encouraged U.S. companies to form joint R&D ventures for the purpose of developing and commercializing new technology. The act also established the Advanced Technology Program (ATP) within the National Institute of Standards and Technology (NIST) of the Department of Commerce (DOC). ATP supports long-term, risky R&D projects in the interests of fostering economic growth.

The Defense Conversion Reinvestment and Transition Assistance Act of 1992 also actively encouraged industry R&D partnerships. It established the Technology Reinvestment Project (TRP), to be administered by the Advanced Research Projects Agency (ARPA) of the Department of Defense. This several-hundred-million-dollar initiative focused public resources on the development of dual-use technology—that is, R&D of benefit to both industry and national defense.

The enactment of the NCRA was a watershed event. But even before 1984, Congress and federal and state agencies had been involved in the formation of EPRI, GRI, and MCC. For example, the initiative to form EPRI came originally from Joseph Swidler, chairman of the Federal Power Commission. And the electric power industry had been under pressure to form its own consortium or be preempted by Congressional initiative. In 1971, Senators Warren Magnuson and Ernest Hollings had introduced legislation calling for the establishment of a federal agency to conduct R&D for the electric power industry, to be funded through a tax on the utilities.

The proposal to form SEMATECH was strongly supported by the Department of Defense. Studies by three other government agencies—the National Science Foundation, the Congressional Budget Office, and Congressional Research Services—also favored SEMATECH's creation. Other government departments were consulted and approved, and federal legislation to provide government funding for SEMATECH was enacted and signed into law by President Reagan in December 1987.

Escalating R&D Costs. In the 1970s and 1980s, rising R&D costs provided a significant inducement for corporations to form consortia for purposes of cost-sharing. The cost of semiconductor design and manufacture would continue to escalate, taking it beyond the point at which any one company could afford the requisite R&D investment. This trend was underscored by Gordon Moore, cofounder of Intel with Robert Noyce, in an article in *Electronics Magazine.* Moore extrapolated on a log-log scale the increasing number of components that were being placed on an integrated circuit. He found that the number doubled every three years, and would amount to sixty-four thousand by 1975. Extrapolations to the year 2000 and beyond had enormous implications for the costs of chip design and the building of a new semiconductor manufacturing plant—the price tag would be more than $1 billion. The current willingness of competitors such as IBM, Toshiba, and Siemens to collaborate in a $1 billion joint venture to develop a next-generation 256 megabit chip is testimony to the influence of astronomical development costs on R&D sourcing arrangements.[6]

Changing Notions of Competitive Advantage. The escalation of R&D costs has led in many companies to the reformulation of ideas about competitive advantage, core competencies, and proprietary technologies. Consequently, it has changed R&D sourcing strategies. Dr. Pallab Chatterjee, president of personal productivity products at Texas Instruments, has stated:

> We are looking at where our competitive advantage lies and what competencies we absolutely must preserve. We won't outsource these, but we will procure related competencies externally. As the concept of *virtual* integration of companies gains favor over that of *vertical* integration, people are getting more focused on what competencies are essential to their competitive advantage. As you focus, you are willing to let go the competencies that lie outside those areas.
>
> On equipment, we buy all our equipment. We are much better off buying as standard a piece of equipment as possible. Availability, cost, and global servicing are much more important than having proprietary equipment. The way we integrate the process and the way we control our factories, that's where our competitive advantage lies.[7]

Commenting in 1994, Dr. Daniel Fleming, director of external development in IBM's microelectronics division, said:

> In the early '60s there were new discoveries every day. You could differentiate in a variety of ways, and cost was not a factor. The overriding factor was what functions could you produce. The goal was to get there before somebody else. Now there are a lot of people in many countries that are capable of working at the leading edge of technology. The limiting factor is economically driven. Consortia can help to get it for you for less money. Now, in semiconductors, we are increasingly moving toward differentiation being at the design level and not the technology level; that is, the architecture for particular applications. We can keep the architecture proprietary at least within a small group by forming alliances.[8]

At IBM, the design of proprietary semiconductor manufacturing equipment was once considered to be an important contributor to product superiority. In the early 1980s, however, IBM's management concluded that developing its own equipment could no longer be justified in terms of either return on investment or competitive advantage.[9] But it became critically important to IBM that a strong domestic semiconductor manufacturing-equipment industry be preserved. Accordingly, IBM gave full support to the formation of SEMATECH, through which the cost of strengthening the manufacturing-equipment sector could be shared with other firms in the computer and semiconductor industries.

Ideas about core competencies and proprietary technologies vary across industries. In industries that are regulated monopolies—gas and electric power, for example—the level of interfirm rivalry is relatively low, as is the opportunity to gain a competitive advantage through the development and use of proprietary technology. The R&D agendas for consortia serving those industries, then, are not likely to be restricted to precompetitive technology domains, however that may be defined by member companies. Conversely, in industries in which firms compete domestically or globally, the value of proprietary technology is likely to be high. Accordingly, R&D consortia in those industries will limit their work to technologies with little or no proprietary value, or will share the cost of developing proprietary technology in a closed alliance with a limited number of partners.

Multilevel Competition. Along with changing notions of competitive advantage comes a growing recognition that competition takes place on different levels. R&D to gain competitive advantage at the interfirm level may be conducted internally and/or through joint ventures. In comparison, R&D to achieve a competitive advantage in interindustry and international rivalries may be conducted by consortia.

Thus at one level, the firm may be the competitive unit—Ford versus General Motors versus Chrysler. On a higher level, the competitive unit may be the domestic industry—the electric power and gas industries competing for a share of the domestic energy market. On a still higher level, industries in one nation may compete against those in another—U.S., Japanese, and European computer giants or automotive manufacturers contending for shares of the world market. In interindustry and international rivalries, the competitive unit includes not only those firms that serve end-product markets, but the entire industry infrastructure—suppliers, distribution channels, university and government research sources, and academic institutions that train the stream of scientists and technicians to carry the industry forward. This recognition that competition is multilevel is one factor that has changed R&D sourcing patterns.

The Role of Consortia in Corporate R&D Sourcing

Given escalating technology costs and the redefinition of core competencies, external R&D sourcing is now accounting for an increasing portion of industrial R&D budgets. Commenting on the trend toward outsourcing, Dr. Chatterjee noted:

> In general there is a shift toward the outsourcing of research. First, there is an emphasis in corporations on R&D connectivity to the business, effectiveness, relevance, and all of those words, and getting a return on the R&D investment. That brings internal R&D closer to the product people. So then there is the question: how do you fill the gap of the longer-term horizon, the work that many of the research people used to be doing. In TI, we have tried to use external funds such as those from ARPA and others to fund longer-range research, but even those budgets are going down. The easiest way to replace these monies is through outsourcing. Outsourcing tends to be for longer-term work and the internal work is focused more on product development. We are also sorting out, in a more discriminating way, what we think is proprietary and what we think we are willing to share with other companies.[10]

And speaking of IBM's experience, Dr. Fleming stated:

> At IBM we are putting less money into research than we used to and so we are looking around and saying if we're not going to do these things, how are they going to get done. The IBM Microelectronics Division is the only division in the company where basic research is done. In each of the product divisions there is a development function but not so much basic research. In the semiconductor technology area, we are increasing the amount of research that is outsourced. That is not true in the design area. As I said, the design area is much more focused on alliances.[11]

In the United States, external sources of corporate R&D include R&D consortia, closed alliances or joint ventures, government laboratories, for-profit contract research firms, and university research centers. Corporations may turn to R&D consortia for those products and services that fall outside the domain of interfirm competition. That would include technology that is focused on industry-wide issues, such as environmental health and safety and the quality and availability of essential national resources; technology that supports a competitive advantage at the interindustry and international levels; industry infrastructure-building; and the development of industry standards.

R&D joint ventures among a limited number of partners often serve as product development vehicles when R&D costs and risks are higher than any one firm is willing to assume, and/or when such arrangements bring together complementary technical expertise and market strengths.

Such partnerships may be the preferred development vehicle for proprietary R&D when gaining a competitive advantage is the key objective. In this domain, the appropriability of R&D results may be maximized first, by confining development work to resources drawn from the partner firms and second, by building up market position to preempt competition. One example is the IBM-Siemens-Toshiba alliance to develop a semiconductor capable of storing 256 million bits of data, announced in July 1992. As was reported in *Business Week,*

> It has to be the alliance of all alliances: On July 13, a deal lasting eight years or more and worth up to $1 billion was announced by IBM, Toshiba, and Siemens. They are, in order, the world's biggest computer company and chipmaker, Japan's second-largest chipmaker, and Europe's No. 3 semiconductor house.
>
> The three companies are joining forces to develop a semiconductor technology so daunting and expensive that none dared risk it alone. The goal is a 21st century chip on whose tiny silicon surface will be etched what amounts to a street map of the entire world. Those electronic streets—lines just 0.25 milicrons wide, 400 times thinner than a human hair—will link some 600 million transistors. When the chips become available around 1998, each will store 256 million bits of data, or about two copies of everything that Shakespeare wrote.[12]

U.S. universities provide a smorgasbord of scientific research programs from which industrial companies may choose, depending on their needs and interests. Many centers take on customized research assignments funded by individual companies. For example, the Massachusetts Institute of Technology is home to more than sixty laboratories and centers, many of which are funded by corporate partners that benefit from a stream of research results in the form of technical papers and conferences. Included in MIT's roster of centers are the Artificial Intelligence Laboratory, the Center for Information Systems Research, the Center for Transportation Studies, and the Electric Power Systems Engineering Laboratory.

At Stanford University, the Center for Integrated Systems (CIS) funds seed research in areas such as factory automation and modeling and portable telecommunications systems. Multidisciplinary in nature, CIS research involves about thirty Stanford faculty members and more than one hundred Ph.D. students in fields such as computer science, applied physics, electrical engineering, and materials science. Successful results lead to further funding, usually by government agencies like ARPA, the Department of Energy (DOE), and the Office of Naval Research (ONR).

Potentially substantial contributors to corporate R&D are the more than three hundred national laboratories that operate under the aegis of six government departments, with combined budgets in excess of $18 billion in 1994. In 1992, three weapons labs alone—Sandia, Lawrence Livermore, and Los Alamos—had research budgets of over $3.5 billion.[13] Under cost-cutting pressure now that the Cold War is over, national labs are searching for new missions. In particular, they anticipate contributing new commercializable technology through industry funding. Thus DOE has launched CRADA (Cooperative Research and Development Agreements), an initiative designed to foster cooperative agreements between industry and DOE's twenty-nine labs. As of 1994, hundreds of agreements had been negotiated with both small entrepreneurial companies and industrial giants like Texas Instruments, Motorola, Baxter Healthcare, and the Big Three automakers.[14] CRADA ventures may well have the potential for developing patentable proprietary technology of benefit to corporate funders in the pursuit of competitive advantage.

The Role of Consortia in Government R&D Programs

Like the private sector, the federal government uses multiple R&D sourcing patterns in which consortia arrangements play a significant part. Large government funders of R&D consortia include the Department of Defense, the Department of Commerce, the Department of Energy, and the National Science Foundation. In the context of government-funded R&D programs, consortia are usually perceived as useful vehicles for what may be called second-stage development work—the implementation of new technical concepts in the form of software programs, hardware, and related equipment. (Stage-one research, developing and demonstrating new concepts, is regarded largely as the domain of university research centers and corporate laboratories.)

Government agencies will sometimes take the initiative in forming R&D consortia. In 1989, concerned about the sharply escalating cost of new semiconductor manufacturing plants, together with the three-year average life of the facilities, ARPA initiated its Microelectronics Manufacturing Science & Technology (MMST) program. What was needed were in-situ process sensors and a comprehensive computer-integrated manufacturing system (CIM) to enable real-time process control. The initial research was cofunded by ARPA, the Air Force's Wright Laboratory, and Texas Instruments (TI). Work was conducted by TI working with research centers at Stanford and MIT and with several semiconductor equipment suppliers. ARPA, TI, and the Air Force each contributed approximately one-third of the $80 million cost of the project. The first phase was completed in 1994, with the demonstration of new concepts in semiconductor fabrication to meet ARPA's objectives. In a second phase, ARPA's program manager interested SEMATECH in carrying the work forward to the development of software and equipment. MMST is an example of work undertaken at ARPA's initiative and moved through two phases using different R&D vehicles.

Another example of government-initiated ventures is the Investment Casting Cooperative Agreement (ICCA) formed in 1993. ARPA saw a need to reduce the cost of super-alloy and titanium precision metal castings, which are used in military aircraft engines and to cut the cycle time from the design to the production of airfoil and structural castings. This is a collaborative venture of aircraft engine builders and their castings suppliers. Consortium members include General Electric's Aircraft Engine Division and Pratt & Whitney Aircraft Engine Company; their castings suppliers, Precision Casting Corporation and Howmet; and Universal Energy Systems, a software company in Dayton, Ohio. Also involved are the University of Alabama, MIT, and NIST. The objective is to develop a casting simulation computer code to link designers at the aircraft engine companies with their suppliers. The project is funded at $12 million, with ARPA contributing half the cost over six years.

NIST's Advanced Technology program (ATP), which is focused on U.S. industrial development, provided $556 million over the four-year period 1990 to 1994 in support of 177 R&D projects. Thirty-five percent of the sixty-one awards and 64 percent of the total funding of $357 million went to joint ventures involving a total of 372 organizations, of which 112 were classified as small business—firms with under five hundred employees. The 2mm program is illustrative. Aware of the funding opportunities available through ATP, eight small, noncompeting technology suppliers to the U.S. auto industry formed the Auto Body Consortium (ABC) in 1991. These companies were providers of high-tech assembly-line equipment, tooling, and systems integration to Ford, General Motors, and Chrysler. In 1992, ABC teamed up with General Motors, Chrysler, the University of Michigan, and Wayne State University to apply for NIST funding for ten related projects aimed at reducing dimensional variation in autobody assembly to less than 2 millimeters. In 1992 the team received a three-year, $5 million grant, to be matched by $7 million from the ABC companies and the two car manufacturers. NIST's portion of the funding supported only the research component of the program, conducted by the two universities.

The 2mm program has now been implemented in several auto and truck assembly plants. A reduction in dimensional variation was achieved

in 44 weeks at Chrysler's Jefferson plant, which produces the Jeep Chero-
kee, and with improved tools and techniques, in just fifteen weeks at GM's
Shreveport assembly plant. At GM's Linden, New Jersey, plant levels of
variation are now running at 1.74 mm. The two car companies estimate
the payback period on their investment to be less than one year, and the
ABC companies stand to profit from the sale of newly designed assembly-
line equipment and tooling.

According to Donald Holtz, director of advanced development at Per-
ceptron, one of the eight ABC member companies,

> We're a small company—100 people—but our U.S. auto company customers are
> depending on us to keep them globally competitive in dimensional variation and
> machine vision. To do that we need access to world class researchers and the
> investment support to conduct the necessary high risk R&D. The ATP provides
> both, and is the only vehicle that does.[15]

In addition to funding such consortia, government agencies play a role
in coordinating the broad array of research being done in many fields,
through interagency forums that bring together representatives of university research centers, national laboratories, industry R&D facilities, and
consortia.

As in industry, R&D consortia play a key role in government programs
for the advancement of technology. They are perceived as vehicles for
doing contract research and for sharing with industry the costs of national
economic development, infrastructure-building, and R&D in environmental health and safety. In general, however, they are not perceived by
government as a source of technological breakthroughs. University research centers and industrial laboratories are seen as more likely sites for
scientific leaps. Instead, consortia are seen as consensus-driven organizations with relatively short time horizons and lower risk tolerance than
other R&D sources. They are perceived as serving as good vehicles for
taking research through the development stage and into practice.[16]

The discussion that follows considers the roles of R&D consortia in Japan
and Europe, for purposes of comparison with those of R&D consortia in
the United States. Available information suggests that consortia in Japan
and Europe play quite different roles from U.S. consortia. In Japan, R&D
collaboration serves primarily as a vehicle for sharing complementary
technology among consortia members, for purposes of fostering corporate
diversification. In Europe, major consortia were formed as pan-European
instruments of public policy, to build Europe's strength in global markets,

protect its home markets, and contribute to national technical and economic development.

It should be noted that data on Japan and Europe come from secondary sources and not from first-hand field observation.

R&D CONSORTIA IN JAPAN

Gibson and Rogers trace the origins of the modern research consortium to industry-oriented alliances formed in England as early as 1917. They were established with partial funding from the British government's Department of Scientific and Industrial Research, to meet the market threat of German competitors.[17]

Drawing on the British model, Masao Sugimoto, director of the Ministry of International Trade and Industry's (MITI) mechanical engineering laboratory, promoted the idea of forming comparable alliances of Japanese companies as vehicles for industry-wide research and development. Japan's first R&D consortium, a collaborative venture of automotive air-filter manufacturers, was founded in 1956. Passage of the Engineering Research Association Act in 1961 by the Japanese Diet gave impetus to the rise of R&D consortia, called ERAs or TRAs (technology research associations), across a range of industries. The act permitted joint research programs under Japan's antitrust law, and offered tax incentives to encourage their formation. In particular, it allowed TRA members to deduct their membership fees and accelerate the depreciation of two-thirds of their fixed assets for research in the first three years.[18] As of 1992, 128 R&D consortia had registered under the act; of that number, 47 have since disbanded.[19]

In the electronics industry, the most notable consortia were the VLSI project to develop the technology for large-scale integrated circuits (1976–1979) and the Fifth Generation Computer Project to develop a working model of an "inference" computer (1982–1992). According to Gibson and Rogers, "MITI pressured the major Japanese electronics companies to form research associations or R&D consortia. The companies were also motivated by their fear of IBM, the U.S. competitor that had dominated their domestic computer market for many years. With each major IBM technological advance, MITI reacted by forming a consortium."[20] VLSI members included Japan's largest electronics companies: NEC, Toshiba, Fujitsu, Hitachi, and Mitsubishi Electric. Funding for the project was budgeted at $312 million over the four-year period, over a third of which came as an interest-free loan from MITI. The total funding was two to three times the combined R&D investment of the five member companies.

The VLSI project was completed in 1979, and consortia members began production of a 64K random-access-memory chip. From just 15 percent of the merchant DRAM market in 1976, the five firms moved to a 70 percent share in 1981 and an 85 percent share in 1986, as chip capacity rose from 4K to 64K to 256K. The attraction of government financial support, pressure from MITI to form electronics industry consortia, and rumors that IBM was developing a new generation of computers based on VLSI circuitry had drawn five intensely competitive firms into a collaborative relationship.[21]

A second consortium, the Fifth Generation Computer Project, was funded at $1.35 billion over ten years, a third of which came from the Japanese government. The alliance included Fujitsu, NEC, Hitachi, Mitsubishi, Toshiba, Matsushita Electric, Oki Electric, Sharp, and NTT, Japan's privatized telecommunications company. To carry out the research, a central research laboratory, the Institute for New Generation Computer Technology (ICOT), was staffed with approximately one hundred scientists. Another two hundred worked on related projects in member-company facilities. While the program did not achieve its goal, one important accomplishment was believed to be the development of a core group of researchers trained in artificial intelligence (AI) design techniques.[22]

The use of R&D consortia to achieve a national competitive advantage, however, is not characteristic of current collaborative endeavors in Japan. Sakakibara's research provides a different picture.[23] Her data base includes 237 government-sponsored R&D consortia formed in Japan between 1959 and 1992. As the following comment by a Japanese industrialist suggests, their primary purpose is to share complementary knowledge, for purposes of diversifying into industries with higher growth rates.

> The major motivation to participate in cooperative R&D is to facilitate the diversification of my company. When we want to enter a new business, it is important to know who else is interested, and to join a government sponsored R&D consortium is, in a sense, to be authorized as a member of "an elite club" on that issue. Once you are recognized as a member, you can get technological knowledge from member companies in other industries. This is the only way to get access to complementary knowledge. Trade associations or academic symposia do not play this role. Mutual dependence is understood among members, therefore when you seek knowledge of others, you are expected to provide your own knowledge in return. In this way knowledge sharing among the companies concerned becomes possible.

It is possible to cooperate with competitors in R&D consortia. However, that is feasible only if participants want to share costs in a non-crucial or non-competing area for all participants, such as recycling problems. We want to avoid knowledge sharing with competitors on the strategically important issues for our company.[24]

This use of collaborative ventures for diversification must be seen in the context of an economy in which a lifetime employment system deters job mobility and the transference of technical knowledge across corporate boundaries. Sakakibara states that in Japan, university and national research laboratories are relatively weak sources of new technology, compared with their counterparts in the United States. Furthermore, the underdevelopment of the market for corporate control renders mergers and acquisitions a less feasible option for diversification. Thus the transfer of resources from mature to growing industries must be essentially internal, aided by knowledge transference through R&D consortia.[25]

R&D CONSORTIA IN EUROPE

One striking feature of the major European R&D consortia is that they are cross-border initiatives. Another is that they are instruments of public policy, funded massively by the European Community, national governments, and industry. These two features must contribute to the complexities of their management and the politicization of R&D agenda setting and governance structures and processes.

The stated purposes of these consortia are to:

- Protect European markets from foreign competition, and avoid dependence on foreign suppliers of technical products.[26]
- Accelerate the growth of European markets,[27] and mold one strong market out of a number of fragmented national markets.[28]
- Strengthen European competitiveness in world markets, and regain Europe's share in the global market for high-tech products.
- Narrow the technology gap among European nations.
- Achieve R&D scale economies.[29]

Six consortia were established to achieve these goals: ESPRIT, formed to pursue information technology; EUREKA, established to work on a wide range of technologies; JESSI, a joint venture of ESPRIT and EUREKA founded to develop leading-edge semiconductor technology and products; RACE, focused on communications technology; BRITE/EURAM, working on materials and manufacturing technology; and Telematics, focused on data-exchange techniques in government, health care, and education. Their missions stress long lead-time research. Operationally, they favor small-nation proposals, small-company involvement, border-crossing research initiatives, and collaboration between academic and corporate technology centers. Descriptions of the three largest European consortia, ESPRIT, EUREKA, and JESSI, follow, with a review of their results and a brief commentary.

ESPRIT (European Strategic Program of Research in Information Technology)

ESPRIT was formed in 1984 to jump-start European semiconductor technology. Its mission is, on the one hand, to increase European chip manufacturers' global market share, and on the other, to protect their domestic markets from foreign competition. European governments are now spending $3 billion a year on ESPRIT, with matching funds from industry.[30] Research domains include microelectronics, software engineering and information processing, advanced business and home information systems, and computer-integrated manufacturing and engineering systems. R&D agenda planning is top-down; the European Union's science secretariat sets research priorities and solicits proposals designed to bring together the best resources from European industry, universities, and independent labs.[31]

While ESPRIT claims credit for more than seven hundred prototypes, tools, and standards, the European Union's court of auditors' 1994 review was critical. The court's essential concern was the paucity of marketable products coming out of Esprit's research program, allegedly the result of ineffective technology transfer and a limiting of R&D to precompetitive stages of development. What was lacking as well, the court said, was a planning process that started with targeted end-product markets in setting the consortium's research priorities.[32] Also noted was an unwillingness on the part of large member companies to exchange data on proprietary hardware and software.[33]

EUREKA (European Research Coordination Agency)

EUREKA was launched in 1985 as a response to President Reagan's Star Wars initiative. Proposed by French President François Mitterrand as a probusiness project with the promise of job creation, it was intended to strengthen him politically. Its projected total cost through 1996 is $15 billion.[33] EUREKA's mission is to support cross-border, precompetitive long-term research for the purpose of recouping Europe's global position in high-technology products.[34] Participants include over thirty-five hundred industrialists, researchers, and public authorities from twenty-two nations and the European Commission.[35] In contrast to ESPRIT, EUREKA's R&D agenda is based on participants' proposals.[36] However, any project must involve at least two companies from each of two different countries,[37] with some bias in favor of smaller companies.[38] A third of EUREKA's funding comes from the governments of member countries and from the European Community (EC).

Of the more than 650 projects in progress in 1994, 60 percent fall into three categories: environmental science, biotechnology and medicine, and robotics. Other areas of research include information technology, new materials, energy, communications, and laser technology.[39] EUREKA's largest funding is for JESSI, its joint venture with ESPRIT, a $4.6 billion, eight-year initiative in semiconductor technology.[40]

EUREKA carries the burden of two major failures. The first is the $740 million effort to develop high-definition television (HDTV) standards for Europe. Work in this field continues under EUREKA's ADTT (Advanced Digital Television Technologies) project, and is funded for a third of EUREKA's current budget, $320 million over thirty months. The second is JESSI's effort to develop a 64 megabit DRAM computer chip, a project with accumulated costs of $3.6 billion as of 1993.[41]

JESSI (Joint European Submicron Initiative)

Launched in 1989, according to plan, JESSI was to be funded by $2.4 billion—25 percent from the EC, 25 percent from national governments, and 50 percent from industry members. It has suffered chronic funding shortages, however; both the EC and the national governments have stinted on their commitments. One large member company, Philips Electronics, withdrew in 1991.[42] Then, Siemens' decision to join with Toshiba and IBM in 1992 in a billion-dollar closed alliance to develop semiconductors with a storage capacity of 256 million bits of data created a political uproar at JESSI.[43]

From the start, Europe's large semiconductor manufacturers seem to have had less than comfortable relations with each other in this consortial context. At first, Siemens of Germany and Philips of the Netherlands fought (unsuccessfully) to bar SGT-Thomson, the French electronics giant, from membership. Then, when Fujitsu purchased a controlling interest in the British company ICL, ICL was expelled from JESSI.[44]

In spite of Europe's investment in semiconductor technology, its share of the world market for semiconductors has continued to erode, from an estimated 17 percent in 1978 to 7.5 percent in 1995,[45] a year when Europe accounted for an estimated 19.6 percent of world consumption of semiconductors.[46] The world market for semiconductors in 1995 was estimated at $152 billion.[47] As for semiconductor manufacturing-equipment, in that year Europe held an estimated 6.7 percent of a $30.5 billion world market share, and accounted for 9.6 percent of worldwide purchases.[48]

In Sum

Overall, European consortia working in high technology areas have been credited with producing some good research and fostering a new spirit of cooperation among European companies, and between industry and university research centers.[49] But at the same time, they have been faulted for the paucity of marketable products emanating from their research programs.[50] In one survey, only 17 percent of EUREKA's corporate participants claimed they had significantly improved their competitiveness as a result of the consortium's R&D.[51]

Funding shortages and budget cuts,[52] bureaucracy,[53] more broadly "government meddling in industrial affairs,"[54] and research not addressed to market needs have been problems.[55] In addition, the European Union's science secretariat has been criticized for favoring ESPRIT proposals from smaller, poorer countries, presumably with less to contribute than the larger, better developed countries.[56] At the same time, the union's court of auditors faulted ESPRIT for lack of participation by small companies.[57]

But there is reason to believe that the real problems are more basic. First, European R&D consortia seem to struggle with conflicting political and technical goals. One such conflict is between technology development per se and nation development. Another is between basic research and end-product development, still another between benefiting smaller companies in awarding R&D grants and drawing on the technology of larger companies.

Finally, the record reflects some degree of incongruity between the interests of the European Union and those of its large multinational companies. A major goal of the European Union is to break down trade barriers, grow internal markets for European-made products, and at the same time increase Europe's competitiveness in world markets. The primary means to this end is perceived as cross-border collaboration in basic research and end-product development. However, large European high-tech corporations have a strong interest in protecting their home-country markets; witness the failed effort of Siemens and Philips to keep SGT-Thomson out of JESSI.

As for the alleged lack of marketable products coming out of ESPRIT, EUREKA, and JESSI, one reason may be that the large member companies do not perceive consortia as a conducive environment for the development of competitive technology. They may be more prone to undertake proprietary product development in their own laboratories, or in closed alliances in which the results of their investment are more appropriable. It is not surprising, then, that Philips withdrew from JESSI, or that Siemens formed an alliance with IBM and Toshiba to pursue development of leading-edge semiconductor technology.

SUMMARY

In the United States the R&D consortium is a relatively new form of enterprise, dating back to the formation of the Electric Power Research Institute in 1973. Conditions that have led to its emergence include:

- external threats, e.g., Japanese ascendancy in the world markets for semiconductors and semiconductor manufacturing equipment, or the Arab oil embargo of 1973;
- the development of national R&D agendas, e.g., environmental health and safety and product interoperability standards;
- a favorable government climate, as evidenced by the passage of the National Cooperative Research Act (1984) and by federal support for consortia such as EPRI, GRI, and SEMATECH;
- escalating R&D costs, which increase the attractiveness of collaboration on noncompetitive research for purposes of cost-sharing;
- a recognized need to build industry supply and market infrastructures for growth and competitive advantage in interindustry and international competition;
- a trend toward outsourcing in response to escalating R&D costs and narrowed delineations of corporate proprietary technology.

In this context, R&D consortia fill a particular niche in performing noncompetitive research, industry infrastructure development, and a range of other functions. In addition, they have come to play key roles as R&D

resources in international competition, and in some instances interindustry competition. In government-funded programs, R&D consortia serve as vehicles for sharing with industry the costs of national economic development, national infrastructure building, and environmental protection.

U.S. R&D consortia are players in an elaborate network of R&D resources that serve the needs of both industry and government for advanced technology, national defense, and national economic development. While university research centers, national labs, and industrial laboratories may serve better as sources of basic research, R&D consortia fill an important role in the development of new technology. Yet even this broad generalization is not without its exceptions.

Japanese R&D consortia, with significant government funding, have helped Japan to build a national competitive advantage in the world market for semiconductors. Currently a major objective of Japanese consortia is the sharing of complementary knowledge among consortium members, for purposes of corporate diversification.

European R&D consortia seem to have been formed largely for defensive reasons. Thus large-scale collaborative efforts such as ESPRIT I, II, and III, EUREKA, and JESSI seek to foster cross-border collaboration in research and product development, for purposes of strengthening European firms against U.S. and Japanese competitors, particularly in the European markets. The results have not been impressive. Shortfalls in performance may well result from mission ambivalence—that is, conflicts between political objectives and technology-development goals. Furthermore, the interests of Europe's large multinational companies may not be totally congruent with the economic goals of the European Community.

Clearly, the roles R&D consortia play in their respective national economies have been shaped significantly by idiosyncratic national needs, government policies, R&D infrastructures, competitive norms, and country or region economic institutions.

CHAPTER 7

In Theory

Existing theories of collective action are based largely on observations of social, communal, and political collaboration: for example, environmental interest groups, industry lobbies, international alliances, labor unions, and farming communities.[1] Thus the focus of theoretical attention has been largely on the provision of public or collective goods—that is, goods that cannot be withheld from anyone, whether or not they have contributed to its production. "Selective goods"—benefits that may accrue to group members and be denied to others—have been treated largely as by-products; they may serve to attract and hold group members who might not collaborate if the public or collective good were the group's sole product.[2]

R&D consortia have not yet been studied by economists, sociologists, and political scientists for what they might contribute to a theoretical understanding of collective action. Thus the purpose of this chapter is to examine the relevance of the current theory of collective action to R&D consortia, and to see how it might be extended based on consortia experience.

The relevant theory, developed largely by Olson and Hardin, may be summarized as follows. A collective good is likely to be provided if the economic gain is great enough for one party or group that it alone would be willing to pay the full cost.[3] Others may join the group if the net benefits to them of contributing to the collective effort are positive, or if some attractive by-product benefits are available only through membership. Noneconomic benefits—for example, the psychic rewards of belonging—may be relevant in small groups, but may decrease in importance for larger groups.

Some individuals may elect not to join, but seek instead to expropriate the benefits of collective action as free riders. For example, if a nation's major oil producers were to lobby for controls on oil imports, small independent producers would gain from the effort, even if they did not contribute to it. Their participation might be induced, however, by certain selective benefits, such as all-expenses-paid trips to the nation's capital to join in the lobbying effort. Free-riding might also be eliminated if all industry members were to agree at the outset to participate in the campaign and pay their share of the cost—an unlikely event, given the context. More likely the major firms would perceive the net benefit of import controls to be sufficiently great that they would be willing to underwrite lobbying costs, free-riding by the independents notwithstanding.

Game theory has contributed to an understanding of the respective stakes of the individual and the group in collective endeavors. In particular, the Prisoner's Dilemma has been used extensively to demonstrate that while acting collusively may produce the greatest total benefit for the group, it may not do so for any one individual.[4] The Prisoner's Dilemma is the story of two prisoners suspected of committing a crime for which the police lack proof. When interrogated separately, each prisoner is offered the same deal: "If you confess, you will get off with only three months in jail, but your partner will get ten years. If he also confesses, then each of you will get five years. If neither of you confesses, we will convict you of the illegal possession of firearms, and that carries a sentence of one year in jail."

Clearly, though the last outcome is not optimal for either individual, it would be the best outcome for the pair. However, if one chooses to confess and the other does not, the one who does not faces ten years in jail. In the case of a one-event choice, a single or a joint confession is the more likely outcome. Thus the prisoners' decisions may well hinge on any plans they may have to continue as partners in crime after serving their sentences. As Axelrod has demonstrated, the pair may arrive at an optimal group solution only if the game is iterative—that is, if successive moves lead ultimately to a recognition of their mutual dependence.[5]

Current theory also holds that large groups will be less effective than small ones, on the grounds that:

> The larger the group, the smaller the share of the total benefit going to any individual, [and] the less the likelihood that any small subset of the group, much less any single individual, will gain enough from getting the collective good to bear the burden of providing even a small amount of it.[6]

This conclusion also follows from the proposition that the larger the group, the more difficult it is to carry out its collective objective, and the easier it becomes for each individual to "leave it to George." Hardin cites Hume, as follows:

> Two neighbors may agree to drain a meadow, which they possess in common; because 'tis easy for them to know each others mind; and each must perceive that the immediate consequence of this failing in his part is the abandoning of the whole project. But 'tis very difficult, and indeed impossible, that a thousand persons shou'd agree in any such action; it being difficult for them to concert so complicated a design, and still more difficult for them to execute it; while each seeks pretext to free himself of the trouble and expense, and wou'd lay the whole burden on others.[7]

On the other hand, certain collective tasks may only be carried out by large groups—for example, lobbying against gun control. The larger the group, the lower may be the average cost per member of producing a collective good without diminishing its value to any one member.[8] Furthermore, theoreticians conclude that there is a tendency for larger group members to bear a disproportionate burden of the total cost. Larger group members may be willing to subsidize smaller ones insofar as the former place a higher value on the collective good.[9]

Finally, the academic literature on collaboration identifies a tendency on the part of groups to underproduce the output of collective goods—that is, to provide lesser amounts than would be in their common interest. The larger the group, the greater the tendency to suboptimize.[10] The proffered explanation is that because the collective good is freely available, large group members realize less than the value of what they pay for. By the same token, the amount of the collective good that members receive free reduces their incentive to provide more at their own expense.

How do these constructs apply to R&D consortia, and to what extent may existing theory be augmented if the reference base is extended to include R&D consortia? The discussion that follows describes the consortium context for purposes of theoretical explorations and then considers the incentives firms have for participating in a collaborative endeavor. Succeeding sections look at the relevance of existing theory to R&D consortia with regard to the influence of membership size on group effectiveness, and at the matter of suboptimization. The role of the core group in consortium formation and governance is the subject of the final section.

THE CONTEXT OF THE CONSORTIUM

As noted in chapter 1, R&D consortia produce a range of products that may be classified as collective, selective, and proprietary. *Collective prod-*

ucts, such as technology for improving the quality of the environment or the development of an industry supply infrastructure, are available to all, consortia members and nonmembers alike. The extent to which any one party benefits does not diminish the benefits that may accrue to others. *Selective products* are R&D achievements made available to individual member firms for such purposes as advancing operations technology, training personnel, and developing new products; their benefits are not easily accessible to nonmembers. Like collective products, any and all members may benefit from a selective product without lessening its value to any one member. *Proprietary technology* is intended to be appropriable by members only, and is usually undertaken to gain some margin of competitive advantage at the level of the firm, as in the case of the IBM-Toshiba-Siemens coalition, or of USCAR, a consortium of Ford, General Motors, and Chrysler. Unlike collective and selective products, the more widely proprietary technology is shared, the less its value to any individual possessor. The development of proprietary products is typically the primary objective of R&D alliances among a limited number of competing firms, but it may also be part of the agenda of consortia such as Bellcore and MCC, which are engaged in developing a full range of collective, selective, and proprietary products.

R&D alliances are formed to share among noncompeting firms the high costs of developing proprietary technology and/or complementary R&D resources. They may also be formed by competing firms, if each may anticipate profits greater than those it might realize acting on its own. Such an outcome could result from R&D cost-sharing, from market growth, or from gaining market share at the expense of nonmember competitors.

As was described in chapter 1, the classification of consortia products as collective, selective, and proprietary is roughly paralleled by the classification of consortia themselves, which may be described as nonexclusive, exclusive, or closed. *Nonexclusive consortia* tend to focus on technology for both collective and selective use by a broad membership. *Exclusive consortia* also pursue selective technology, but they are organized to advance the interests of some specific group—for example, domestic firms. Other firms are excluded by class—for instance, all non-U.S. firms. *Closed consortia* seek to develop proprietary technology, often to enhance members' market shares in interfirm and/or international competition. Among U.S. consortia, the Electric Power Research Institute (EPRI) and the Gas Research Institute (GRI) are nonexclusive. SEMATECH, the Semiconductor Research Institute (SRC), and the Microelectronics and Computer

Technology Corporation (MCC) are exclusive, insofar as their doors are closed to foreign firms, except for Canadian corporations. Bellcore and USCAR are closed coalitions.

Another way of thinking about consortia is in terms of their membership, which typically includes—and in fact, may be limited to—a core group, as is the case with USCAR and Bellcore. Coalitions with larger memberships will include a subset of noncore members as well. In either case, some core group typically takes the initiative in forming the consortium, and is largely responsible for establishing its policies. EPRI and GRI are good examples. Other beneficiary constituencies may include a nonmember clientele—that is, the consortium's paying customers. (In 1995, for example, 23 percent of Bellcore's revenues came from nonowner customers in the telecommunications industry.) Finally, a substantial constituency are free riders, those who benefit from consortia R&D but do not contribute to it.

These three taxonomies will be put to work in the discussion that follows, which considers why consortia are formed and why some firms elect to participate and some do not; how a consortium's purpose is related to matters of size, membership policy, and operational form; and finally how core groups, noncore members, and nonmembers help to formulate and advance a consortium's objectives.

THE RATIONALE FOR COLLABORATION

In theory, the economic rationale for the formation of a collaborative group is the anticipation of gain by some member or core group—a greater gain than if the member or core group were to undertake the same mission independently.[11] The discussion that follows explores the benefits and costs of collective action.

The Benefits of Collaboration

Potential gains from collaborative endeavors may emanate from cost sharing, the sharing of complementary technology, and the reduction of risk. Cost-sharing opportunities are prime motivators in the formation of consortia for the development of collective and selective R&D products in noncompetitive domains. Sharing complementary technical knowledge is often the purpose of consortia that are formed to develop proprietary technology to advance competitive interests. Such alliances provide transitioning opportunities for firms moving into new fields of technology or diversifying into new businesses. For example, Sakakibara's study of government-sponsored cooperative R&D projects in Japan indicates that by far the most important objective of those consortia is internally generated diversification through the sharing of complementary knowledge.[12]

Risk-reduction opportunities provide an incentive for collaboration on large-scale projects with a relatively high degree of uncertainty. Examples are the IBM-Toshiba-Siemens joint venture[13] and Boeing's partnership with four leading European aerospace firms in the design and construction of large-capacity passenger planes.[14]

Another form of risk reduction that a collaborative venture provides is the opportunity to monitor technological advances in competitors' R&D programs. As Sakakibara notes:

> The risk of not participating in cooperative R&D is another reason to sustain cooperation. In government sponsored R&D consortia, participants can often get access to researchers in national labs and universities, and can get first-hand government information. Firms can also observe what other firms are concerned with, and learn the direction of their research. It is especially important when network externalities of technology are significant, in which the risk of not knowing the direction of a possible industry standard or trend can be a major disadvantage.[15]

The potential for economic gain tends to be augmented by noneconomic motivations, particularly on the part of the core group.[16] Core-group leaders are likely to have a sense of responsibility for the consortium's success, and to value the opportunity to direct a nonprofit enterprise of importance to the nation and the industry. Such motives may have particular weight with top executives of larger member firms, who may see the future of their firms as dependent on the health of the industry at large, and who may personally identify with an industry leadership cohort.

The consortium context, along with trade association meetings, industry/government committees, and social gatherings may also provide networking opportunities. Because these are typically ongoing relationships involving the same cohort, they are likely to foster a greater sense of cooperation and mutual dependence among core-group members, and a more heightened awareness of the effect of one's actions on others, than might be the case for smaller members.[17]

Noneconomic motives seem to have particular weight in a consortium's formative stages. First, there may be little initially on which to base an economic assessment of the value of a collaborative effort to member companies. And second, consortia are often formed out of a sense of industry or national patriotism, to accomplish some overarching purpose associated with crisis events.

With time, however, economic motives take increasing precedence over more ephemeral noneconomic motivations. The original mission may be fulfilled or in sight of fulfillment, or it may be less relevant; and the value of the consortium's output now is more measurable in terms of member ROI. A shift in emphasis from noneconomic to economic motives is typically concomitant with a shift in core-member representation on governance boards, from the CEO level down to senior department heads. The latter, more than their predecessors, respond to departmental performance measures, and must rely on ROI numbers to justify consortium membership fees. Thus while Robert Noyce could rally the computer industry, DOD, and Congress in support of rescuing the U.S. semiconductor manufacturing-equipment sector, his successor at SEMATECH, William Spencer, moved quickly to establish ROI measures of consortium output in order to sustain member support.

In the absence of compelling economic rewards, it is unlikely that noneconomic motives will sustain a collaborative enterprise over the long term. A firm's decision to join a collaborative venture and later to renew its membership annually rests largely on cost-benefit analyses. Furthermore, in assessing potential membership benefits, selective and proprietary product offerings are likely to be given much greater weight than collective R&D, which is freely available to members and nonmembers alike.

The Costs of Membership

The costs of membership include three basic components: membership fees, extraction costs—that is, personnel time and expenditures associated with the acquisition of technology—and implementation costs, or the cost of putting new technology to use. Thus at SEMATECH, the total cost of member involvement includes annual fees, the support of member-company assignees, who work on projects of value to their firms, and the cost of transforming new technology to engineering and production personnel, who are charged with making it operational in manufacturing plants around the world. While annual fees typically vary according to some measure of member revenue, and by implication with the value of membership to the firm, extraction and implementation costs are likely to be less variable, and to impose a proportionally greater burden on small companies than on large ones.

Any cost-benefit assessment of collaboration must be compared with the option of eschewing membership and acquiring consortium products through other channels, such as the supply-industry infrastructure, academic journals, trade associations, and the recruitment of new technical personnel from other firms. While the cost of not joining a collaborative endeavor may be measured in terms of a lag in the acquisition of new technology, the net benefits of free-riding may exceed those of membership status, especially for small companies. One reason is the limited interest of small companies in the range of consortium products, and a resulting unwillingness to support the full R&D agenda. Another is that the cost of extraction and implementation may account for a proportionally larger share of a small firm's total technology acquisition cost, including a membership fee scaled to the firm's size. That is, while annual fees typically vary according to some measure of member revenue, extraction and implementation costs will correlate to a much lesser degree with a firm's size, and will constitute a greater share of the total membership cost for a small firm than for a large one. Finally, the capacity of the small firm to implement new technology may be limited.

The benefits of free-riding are contingent, of course, on the accessibility of new technology through indirect channels. Collective benefits are by definition freely available to all. And some selective benefits may be easily expropriated through industry supply sectors, the trade press, and academic journals. U.S. public policy also favors the free rider: a condition of maintaining a nonprofit tax status is that a consortium make its products quickly available to the public at large, thus enhancing the attractiveness of free-riding.

CONSORTIUM SIZE

The academic literature pays great attention to the influence of size on the effectiveness of collective action. As Hardin notes, "The most controversial issue in the contemporary literature on collective action has probably been that of the effect of size on the likelihood of group success."[18]

Olson contends that individual incentives to collaborate decrease with group size. The larger the group, the smaller the share of benefits for any one individual.[19] And the greater the number of people who must be coordinated, the higher the cost of organizing them effectively.[20] Hardin would amend that hypothesis by redefining group size, not in terms of absolute numbers, but with respect to the size of the core group, defined as "the number of . . . members who, taken as a group themselves, could all benefit if they alone provided the whole group's goods."[21]

What, then, is the effect of size on consortia effectiveness? Among the six consortia that are the primary focus of this study, size seems to have had no effect on the incentives of individual firms to participate, even in the case of large memberships. One reason is that increasing size does not diminish the availability of collective and selective benefits to individual members. Collective and selective products are not a pie of finite size, which must be divided into increasingly smaller slices as the number of member beneficiaries grows. Technical knowledge has the quality, in economists' terms, of "high jointness of supply." As for the effect of group size on organizing costs, clearly the larger the group, the greater the administrative overhead. But to correlate the level of organizing costs with some measure of group effectiveness would be specious.

As EPRI's experience shows, large coalitions may be feasible if the number of potential beneficiaries is large, and the benefits of participation large relative to average cost. Another condition is that the net benefits realizable by core-group members, though not exclusively appropriable, must be sufficiently large to assure the group's willingness to cover most of the costs.

A useful question is what the optimal size of a consortium is, given its mission. For this purpose, one might compare EPRI, with more than seven hundred members, SEMATECH, with eleven members, and USCAR, with three. At EPRI, optimal size is a function first of the revenues needed to support the scale and scope of an R&D program that covers all aspects of electric utility technology, and provides for its delivery in a variety of forms. And second, the limits of optimal size may lie at that point where the marginal cost of recruiting and serving new consortium members exceeds the marginal income provided. Given a fee structure based on member size, the smaller the member, the less the difference between net revenue and recruiting and service costs. Within this constraint, it would seem that EPRI may have as large a membership as it can profitably recruit, with no loss of benefits to members. A larger membership base may support some combination of increased program scale or reduced fee schedule. Furthermore, investment in recruiting is likely to yield a higher payoff if it is focused on the larger utilities, to which membership may also be easier to sell because of a more favorable cost-benefit equation. It is not surprising, then, that EPRI's members include the largest electric utilities in the nation. They represent less than

25 percent of the nation's electric utilities, but account for more than 70 percent of the total retail kilowatt-hours of electricity produced.

The same precepts would apply to SEMATECH. Focused on precompetitive research and development of the U.S. semiconductor manufacturing-equipment infrastructure, SEMATECH might logically be open to any firm, domestic or foreign, that can contribute revenue in excess of recruiting and service costs. The limits currently imposed on SEMATECH—that members be substantially owned and directed by U.S. interests—would seem to remain as a vestigial condition of receiving government funding. (To be fair, however, SEMATECH's members may see little gain in admitting non-U.S. firms, and may perceive some lead-time advantage in excluding competing oligopolies in Europe and Asia.)

USCAR, a consortium of Ford, Chrysler, and General Motors, is of another genre. This alliance illustrates Olson's hypothesis that the more members, the less for each. Conceived to develop technology that will yield the three domestic car makers a competitive advantage in global competition, USCAR's optimal size may be the smallest number of members that is needed to provide the necessary financial support and technical resources to carry out its mission. Any further sharing—say, with foreign competitors that have plants in the United States—would only dilute the market benefits of the consortium without, presumably, adding technical value to the R&D program.

SUBOPTIMIZATION

Do consortia underinvest? If so, what is the evidence and why? As with R&D programs in general, consortia R&D planning processes typically skim off those projects with the highest anticipated payoff and reject others. Thus in a budget-limited planning process, consortia are likely to forgo projects with returns that are attractive, but not good enough to make the cut.

Evidence of suboptimization may also lie in the anecdotal testimony of consortia members that the return on their fee investments (their ROI) may run on the order of 300 to 400 percent. If so, that would certainly raise questions about why more is not invested in consortia R&D. Particularly with regard to spending on *collective* R&D, however, consortia members are likely to adopt satisficing goals. They will do what is necessary to meet the requirements imposed on them by external constituencies and by their directors, in terms of satisfying public demand for service.

In the case of *selective goods,* the estimated ROIs may be misleading if they fail, as they seem to do, to take account of extractive and implementation costs. In any case, member firms are limited in their capacity to absorb and implement technology. Finally, no one member, in spite of realizing high returns on its membership fee, can buy greater amounts of R&D, as it might buy more cost-saving capital equipment. In a consortium environment, increases in the production of R&D are initiated by the membership group, not by the individual member. Accordingly, group decision making focuses on the broad parameters of the consortium's program, on budget levels, and on allocations among technical fields. Fee increases to fund a steady growth in the consortium's R&D program may be supported over the long term.

As in EPRI's Tailored Collaboration program and Bellcore's elective R&D program, however, members can and do initiate and purchase customized research projects. If members increase their consortium payments, the increase is likely to be applied to customized projects rather than to the common R&D agenda. Thus it is largely with regard to the common agenda that consortia tend to suboptimize.

THE CORE GROUP

In addition to supporting and/or amending existing theories of collective action, observations of R&D consortia provide a context for extending ideas about collaborative effort. In particular, they offer opportunities to hypothesize about the dynamics of member relationships.

Each member subset—*core group, noncore members,* and *nonmembers*—plays a distinctive role in the fulfillment of the consortium's mission. In consortia with a small number of members, like Bellcore and SEMA-TECH, the membership *is* the core group. In larger R&D ventures like SRC, EPRI, and GRI, the core group generally represents large member companies and industry trade associations, and is particularly active in high-level governance bodies. Noncore members may participate actively on committees and task forces, contributing to the flow of project proposals and extracting R&D products for their use. Nonmembers are of two types: *free riders* by choice or exclusion and *client firms* that commission customized R&D projects.

The core group usually takes the initiative in forming the consortium. At SRC, the core group included Digital Equipment, Intel, IBM, National Semiconductor, and Advanced Micro Devices—all large firms and members of the Semiconductor Industry Association. Membership in the core group may be consonant with seats on the board of directors. Thus at SRC, ten out of nineteen seats on the board of directors are reserved for representatives of the ten largest fee contributors. At small consortia like Bellcore and SEMATECH, all members are represented on the board of directors.

Beyond giving birth to the collaborative venture, the core group plays other crucial roles. First, the large firms subsidize the small ones.[22] While membership fees typically vary with a firm's size, as may the value of benefits received, the per member cost of producing and distributing R&D product does not vary in proportion to fees paid. Large members contribute more than their unit share of total costs to collective and selective R&D. Such a subsidy may be the cost of sustaining collaboration, and probably of maximizing the membership base within some optimal size range. For example, at SRC, the annual fee for the largest members is in excess of $3 million, while the smallest members pay a minimum of $65,000. Yet all members have equal access to SRC academic research, publications and, for recruiting purposes, to graduate students trained in semiconductor design and manufacture.

Figure 7.1 shows the subsidy graphically. In this construct, the area ABEG represents total consortium costs; ACFG represents total revenue. Note that areas ABEG and ACFG are equal in size. Lines AC and FG represent the annual fees paid by the largest and smallest consortium members, respectively. The line CF is the schedule of fees for members. Thus the area BCD represents the amount by which the larger fee payers subsidize the smaller fee payers, an amount equal to the shortfall DEF.

The core group, identifying as it does with the industry, serves also to keep the agenda focused on R&D of broad relevance—that is, on a collective agenda and widely applicable selective-product development. An example is the recent requirement imposed by directors on EPRI's membership that, under EPRI's Progressive Flexibility program, 30 percent of each member's fee must go to support programs in environmental R&D and basic research. (The other 70 percent may be allocated to any of twelve other programs.) In effect, a tax is imposed on members to support the collective portion of the consortium's programs. The fact that support for environmental R&D and basic research is mandated implies that EPRI's governing bodies deem it unlikely that it would be supported voluntarily if classified as elective work.

Figure 7.1   The Core-Group Subsidy Effect

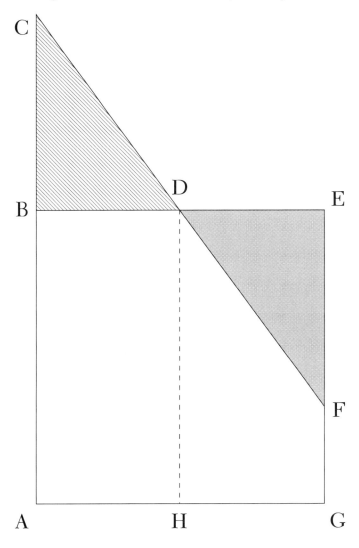

Key:

Large-member subsidy of small member's fees

Shortfall in cost coverage by small members

At the same time, large members tend to use consortium R&D more than small members to serve their needs. The large firms have more resources both to buy such services and to make them operational.

Core-group members tend also to recognize their mutual dependency in ongoing relationships. Thus any thought of withdrawing from collaboration is likely to be attended by concern over the impact of such an action on core-group relationships and on the consortium's membership at large. Also, the threat of secession by one or more large members gives the core group an element of power not possessed by small members.

Noncore members and nonmember R&D customers may be thought of as core-member clients. They provide revenue, articulate market needs, and carry out the consortium's mission, to the extent that they use collective products and provide business for the industry's supply infrastructure. Though free riders do not contribute to the support of a consortium's R&D programs, they may further its collective purpose if the sharing of proprietary knowledge is not at stake. For example, to the extent that the industry's supply infrastructure is strengthened by revenues from the sale of products to free riders, both EPRI and SEMATECH gain. And to the extent that free riders put the consortia's collective and selective R&D to use, their collaborative missions are more fulfilled.

S U M M A R Y

In many respects, observations of R&D consortia tend to bear out existing theories of collective action. As they suggest, the incentives to form a consortium are largely economic, and the initiative for collaborative endeavor typically comes from an individual or core group for whom the anticipated net benefit is estimated to exceed the anticipated total cost of the venture.

Existing theory does not give due weight to the importance of noneconomic incentives for collaboration, however. The R&D consortia experience suggests ways of thinking more critically about the influence of such incentives on decisions to form and/or join collaborative groups. First, noneconomic motives are likely to be more important to members of a core group than to noncore participants. Second, they are likely to assume greater weight in a consortium's formative period than in its maturity.

Existing theory also understates the importance of the availability of selective benefits on decisions to join collaborative endeavors. Current theoretical constructs were developed in the context of political, social, and communal collaboration, with a primary goal the achievement of some collective purpose. In the context of R&D consortia, however, the availability of selective and proprietary benefits is of primary importance. Collective goals may help to enlist broad support, especially in the formative stages, but in the long run the availability of selective R&D products weighs most heavily in any cost-benefit assessment.

Within the R&D consortia on which this study is based, there is no evidence to support existing hypotheses about the influence of size on the effectiveness of collective action. Any perceived differences in effectiveness are attributable to other variables. Consortia do, however, offer clues to the determinants of optimal size. They include, first, the research scale and operational scope required to develop and disseminate some range of R&D products to member firms. A second determinant is the incremental cost of recruiting and serving members versus potential fee revenues. Another is the benefit of enlisting broad support for some collaborative R&D agenda versus the costs, in terms of competitive advantage, of sharing proprietary information.

Further studies of R&D consortia suggest new hypotheses about the dynamics of the relationships among core-group members, noncore members, and nonmembers, including both nonmember customers and free riders. As theory predicts, some core group comprised of industry leaders and other large firms is likely to subsidize the collective effort. And in effective consortia, the core group also fosters overall consortium and industry interests, by assuring the pursuit of collective and selective product research that is of broad relevance to the industry at large. At the same time, large members will tend to bend consortium resources to serve their own interests. They may do so by funding large-scale customized research and by investing heavily in R&D extraction.

Noncore members serve multiple purposes. They contribute incremental revenue to reduce the core group's funding burden, help to shape the R&D agenda, and lend support to the pursuit of the consortium's purposes and strategies. That is, they are under the tent rather than outside it.

Nonmember consortium customers augment the consortium's revenues. Free riders, too, may contribute to the pursuit of collective and selective (but not proprietary) R&D, to the extent that they use consortia-developed industry infrastructures and implement new collective-product technology.

Theories of collective action have important implications for consortium management. They concern membership dynamics, cost-benefit analysis, and optimal size. First, theory draws attention to the essential role a core group plays in the formation and governance of a consortium. It suggests that a consortium's effectiveness may well depend on the quality of its core group. While earlier discussions in this book have focused on *personal* leadership as a critical factor in a consortium's success, theory highlights the importance of *core group* leadership.

One condition of a core group's effectiveness is cohesion around some clear and unambiguous mission with a high net value to each core-group member. Core-group membership should also be representative of the industry's leadership structure—that is, of the technical and market leaders in the sector the consortium has been formed to serve. Identification with broad industry interests helps to assure an R&D agenda that includes collective and selective product development of relevance to both industry and national interests.

Among the consortia on which this study has focused, those that have been most effective in terms of growth, membership recruiting and retention, and mission fulfillment tend to have strong and cohesive core groups. SEMATCH, EPRI, and SRC are good examples. In the other cases, the core group's effectiveness may suffer from divergent interests (GRI), competitive rivalry among core-group members (Bellcore), or mission ambivalence (MCC).

The fact is, not much is known about the dynamics of consortium governance and decision making. The requirements for core-group effectiveness and the dynamics of the relationships among core-group members, noncore members, and nonmembers are not fully understood. Greater understanding of these phenomena could contribute significantly to better formation and management of R&D consortia.

The theoretical constructs developed in this chapter also suggest cost-benefit analysis as an area for further study. How can the full cost of consortium membership, including annual fees and R&D extraction, and implementation costs, be measured? How can the value of member benefits be quantified? How do R&D delivery costs vary across a consortium's product line, and across the member size range? How do the costs members incur for R&D extraction and implementation vary with their size? At what point do the costs of recruiting and serving individual members exceed their membership fees? Precision in cost-benefit-revenue analyses and optimal-size calculations is likely to be difficult to attain. But even an understanding of the critical variables in such calculations would be helpful in consortium management.

Finally, theories of collective action need to be tested and extended. To do so would require a data base broader than this book's, as well as in-depth studies of selected consortia.

CHAPTER 8

■

Conclusions

Since the formation of the Electric Power Research Institute in 1973, R&D consortia have grown in economic importance and become an established part of the national R&D infrastructure. As the preceding chapters have documented, consortia have contributed significantly to the development and diffusion of technology in the industries they serve. They have been effective in building industrial and academic infrastructures. Many have developed new products to meet member-company needs and grow the end markets they serve. Some, EPRI and GRI, for example, have played an active role in the commercialization of new end products. R&D consortia have contributed on a national level as well, to environmental health and safety, defense technology, and national competitiveness. They provide vehicles for cost- and risk-sharing in research and development that are of broad use to the industries they represent, and ultimately to the nation. Consortia serve as forums for the development of strategies for economic growth and national competitiveness, without limiting interfirm competitiveness or imposing a national industrial policy on U.S. industry.

What of the future? Are R&D consortia likely to grow in number, to become increasingly important to the advance of technology? Or will they decline in their role as contributors to technological development and as players in a national R&D network? A reasonable expectation is that consortia are likely to become even more firmly established, as long as the conditions that led to their rise still obtain. Those conditions, noted earlier, are: (1) rapid technological development; (2) escalating research costs; (3) growing use of external R&D sources by corporations; (4) industry-level R&D agendas that are beyond the resources or the self-interest of individual firms; (5) growing use of cost-sharing arrangements between industry and government, for the development of the national economy, the support of the defense establishment, the husbanding of national resources, and the protection of the environment; (6) industry and government funding for those purposes; and (7) a favorable legislative environment.

Even if continued growth of R&D consortia is anticipated, several issues remain. How are consortia likely to evolve as economic institutions? What will be their effect on industrial organization, technological innovation, national investment in new technology, and market growth? Finally, what are the conditions for their success—that is, what will it take to ensure that R&D consortia serve their memberships, their industries, and the nation effectively? These questions are addressed in the discussion that follows.

HOW WILL CONSORTIA EVOLVE?

Three predictions seem reasonable. First, R&D consortia are likely to attract the larger firms in their industries. Second, they will tend to focus on low-risk endeavors with near-term time horizons. Third, R&D collaboration will tend to occur in domains in which standardization offers greater member benefits than differentiation for competitive purposes. These predictions suggest a continuation of existing consortia characteristics.

It is not surprising, for example, that EPRI's members represent 70 percent of the total output of electric power in the United States but only 25 percent of the nation's electric utilities. Nor is it surprising that SEMATECH's members are the largest producers and users of semiconductors in the United States. Large firms may benefit more from a broad R&D agenda. They may realize greater returns on membership fees, given the scale and scope of their businesses, than smaller firms. Certainly they have greater resources for extracting and implementing new technology, as well as greater resources for funding customized research. Finally, large producers are more likely to be able to appropriate consortia output, given their market share positions. At the same time, nonmember firms and their industries at large will benefit from the supply and market infrastructure development consortia foster, and from collaborative work on the national industry and technology agendas—for example, environmental preservation. Except in the case of closed alliances, new technology resulting from R&D consortia is quickly disseminated through supply infrastructures, academic journals, and technical-personnel recruiting.

In general, R&D consortia focus more on development than on research. As was demonstrated early in MCC's history, consortia members show a low tolerance for projects with time horizons longer than three years. One reason, obviously, is that the benefits of short-term advances may be realized sooner. Further, development may focus more than research on selective products of benefit to members, and is more appropriable than long-term research, the results of which are difficult to contain within the consortium over extended periods. Furthermore, given the consensus-driven nature of the R&D planning process, decision making will tend to favor low-risk, near-term projects. The planning process may also reflect the primacy of short-term performance measures in member firms.

Finally, it must be recognized that R&D consortia are just one link in the technology infrastructure. The basic long-term research on which consortia feed comes largely out of university research centers and corporate and government laboratories; it is often funded by governments and corporations as well as by R&D consortia. Those institutions give greater priority to long-term advances in technology, and the reputations of their researchers are built on technological breakthroughs. Thus, the role of R&D consortia seems to be defined by their markets, the corporate and government consumers of technological development.

As has been noted, firms will tend to use consortia to gain the benefits of standardization, but will avoid collaboration where product or service differentiation yields a competitive advantage. The advantages of standardization brought the United States' leading semiconductor manufacturers and users together in SEMATECH, to build up the equipment manufacturing infrastructure. None of those firms would have benefited by differentiation in the design of semiconductor manufacturing equipment. Similarly, standardized power-generation and distribution equipment developed through collaboration is more readily available and of lower cost than equipment tailored to idiosyncratic user requirements. This is an important reason for the existence of GRI and EPRI.

Finally, what is the outlook for multinational R&D consortia? It is probably good. EPRI and GRI have already admitted foreign firms. Bellcore, too, has collaborative relationships with foreign firms. Multinational consortia are most likely to grow for purposes of developing collective and selective R&D products for national infrastructures—for example, energy and telecommunications services, and perhaps health-care and educational technologies. These are domains in which national governments have a major stake, and are likely to encourage industry R&D

initiatives through funding and conducive regulatory environments. These are also areas that are of low salience in national competitive advantage, compared with electronic components and end products, financial services, and cars. Multinationally organized R&D consortia have an increasingly important role to play as well in standard-setting, as technological advances create a need for global interoperability protocols.

Cross-national collaboration through R&D alliances is also likely to grow in the pursuit of proprietary technology in domains of high salience for global competitive advantage. R&D consortia will continue to be the vehicle of choice when a venture is high in risk or cost, when partners can share complementary technology resources, and when each partner's primary market is different from the others, as in the IBM-Siemens-Toshiba alliance to develop a next-generation semiconductor. In that alliance, the cost- and risk-sharing benefits, the potential for overall market growth, and the opportunity to gain a competitive advantage over nonmembers outweigh the competitive disadvantages of sharing new proprietary technology within the alliance.

ECONOMIC CONSEQUENCES

The growth of R&D consortia is likely to have a number of economic effects. It will tend to foster and/or give impetus to oligopolistic industry structures, industrial deintegration, increases in national R&D investments, and market growth. There is a question, however, whether R&D consortia will tend to dampen innovation and technology-based competition. This and the foregoing assertions are the subject of the sections that follow.

Oligopolistic Industry Structure

As has been noted, the larger firms in an industry tend more often to join consortia than the smaller ones. Thus consortia may serve as vehicles for forging oligopolies, both horizontally and vertically. SEMATECH, for example, helps its members to strengthen their relationships with each other and with the industry's supply infrastructure; to reduce interfirm transaction costs; and to strengthen the United States' competitive posture in global markets without diminishing interfirm rivalry. At the same time, consortial relationships are likely to provide opportunities for gaining competitively useful information, thus fostering a greater degree of strategic interdependence among member firms.

Industrial Deintegration

The prevailing trend toward R&D outsourcing adds impetus to the movement, in the last quarter-century, away from vertically integrated corporate structures, to *virtual integration*.[1] As supplies of materials, components, and end products, as well as a wide range of industrial services are outsourced, vertical structuring gives way. Badaracco and others refer to these developments as the blurring of corporate boundaries.[2]

As this study demonstrates, the collaborative outsourcing of R&D has become an attractive option for noncompetitive technology development and high-cost, high-risk R&D. Furthermore, to the extent that consortium work with industry suppliers takes costs out of interfirm transactions—as it does at SEMATECH—externalizing the sourcing of supplies and equipment gains in attractiveness.

National R&D Expenditure Levels

National R&D expenditures are likely to increase in the future, for one reason because consortia investments in R&D tend often to be leveraged. Consortia partnerships with R&D contractors typically involve cost-sharing investments on the part of the contractors, which presumably would not be made in the absence of the consortium's initiative. In 1992, for example, the Gas Research Institute's $180 million expenditures generated cofunding from commercializing R&D contractors of $84 million. Leveraging occurs in other ways as well. The Semiconductor Research Corporation's investment in academic research at different universities across the nation has attracted state and university funding for new research facilities. In addition, government investments in R&D consortia serve either to reduce the funding burden assumed by corporate members or to expand the R&D agenda, thus stimulating membership recruitment. Finally, the knowledge firms gain through collaborative relationships, of new technology and of other firms' plans for its exploitation, is likely to stimulate R&D spending across competing firms.[3]

Infrastructure Development and Market Growth

There is ample evidence that R&D consortia have contributed significantly to both infrastructure development and market growth in the industries in which they have been active. In many instances, consortia members themselves comprise a substantial market for the products their funding helps to create. One effect is a reduction in market uncertainty on the part of suppliers, which encourages investment in market development. Beyond that, the markets in which consortia members sell are expanded by consortia-generated end products.

Innovation and R&D Competition

Three arguments may be made to support the contention that R&D consortia tend to dampen innovation and R&D competition. First, the consensus-building nature of the R&D planning process forecloses competing ideas. Second, a propensity to take on low-risk projects with near-term time horizons, and a tendency to work toward satisficing goals discourage innovation. Furthermore, there is no evidence of interconsortial R&D competition within industry sectors. In her study of R&D consortia in Japan, Sakakibara makes this observation:

> Cooperation in R&D is associated with risks. The most dangerous risk for participating firms is the risk to R&D competition. Cooperative R&D can lead to collusion in R&D, which discourages R&D investment. Cooperative R&D also tends to lead to technology convergence, and it reduces diversity of research paths. As a result, cooperation in R&D can slow down the speed of innovation, and firms might find themselves behind international competition. Also, through the loss of technology diversity, firms will lose an opportunity to choose different technologies to serve different markets, and can be confined to a single strategy. It is therefore likely that firms have to compete in a single dimension, such as capacity expansion or cost reduction. One of the reasons the Japanese computer industry is not internationally competitive is that cooperative R&D projects among leading computer makers in the 1960s and in the 1970s helped to align their focus on the hardware mainframe computers, and so they did not develop the necessary capabilities to compete in the personal computer segment after distributed processing became dominant in information technology.[4]

To the contrary, it may be argued that U.S. R&D consortia have scored a range of innovative successes, e.g., SEMATECH's development of .35 micron technology for making semiconductors; Bellcore's pioneering research on transmission standards for fiber-optic systems, which resulted in SONET; and EPRI's work on solar cells. The more important consideration, however, is that at least in the United States, the primary loci of technological competition are university research centers, government laboratories, and some corporate laboratories. It may follow, then, that the appropriate role of R&D consortia is to build on these often competing initiatives, to help carry basic research forward into practice. Many consortia do in fact have affiliations with university research centers, and provide supportive funding.

In the author's opinion, consortia per se do not dampen innovation and R&D competition. Levels of innovation and competition result from the character of a nation's entire R&D infrastructure. Furthermore, those infrastructures are at the heart of international R&D competitiveness; they compete with each other for technological leadership. European and U.S. consortia, such as SEMATECH, MCC, and SRC, were formed as instruments of international technological competition.

Yet the charge that R&D consortia tend to dampen innovation is not without merit. It is important for consortia managements to sustain some leading edge of research aimed at breakthroughs that go beyond the fine-tuning of existing scientific bases.

GOVERNMENT POLICY

What conditions will assure and indeed augment the continued contribution of consortia to the companies and industries they serve, and to the U.S. economy? There are two. The first is favorable government policy and constructive government participation in consortia programs. The second is a high level of expertise in the formation and management of consortia.

R&D consortia serve both the public and private sectors. A fundamental issue, then, is whether they are better positioned as instruments of national economic policy, as in Europe, or as an integral part of private enterprise. There are examples of both. The more successful consortia considered in this study, EPRI, SEMATECH, and SRC, have emerged from private-sector initiatives. Certain government-initiated single-purpose collaboratives have achieved success as well, e.g., Japan's VLSI program and single-purpose projects started under ARPA and NIST auspices.

In Europe, however, government-formed consortia like EUREKA, ES-PRIT, and JESSI—all ongoing, massively funded, with broad R&D agendas of national import—have failed to live up to expectations. They have not protected Europe's high-tech home markets, improved ECU competitiveness in world markets, or advanced national economic development, though they were formed under government auspices and operate in accordance with government-established priorities.

In the United States, GRI, more than any other U.S. consortium in this study, was shaped significantly by regulatory and judicial influences with regard to membership composition, funding mechanisms, governance structures and processes, and decision rules relevant to R&D planning.

GRI continues to operate under stipulations that establish the hurdles for R&D project and program approval by FERC. In practice, GRI's management seems to have had to cope with excessive conflict among both internal and external constituencies; undue limitations on the scope of its work; and funding caps.

One tendency evident in consortia in which government has been integrally involved is a multiplicity of goals, some economic, some political, some not completely congruent with member interests. Thus, to warrant approval, GRI's R&D projects must have the potential to benefit primarily *existing* classes of ratepayers. This stipulation precludes projects aimed at developing new markets and new customer sets to their benefit and that of the natural gas industry.

In Europe, consortia such as EUREKA, ESPRIT, and JESSI, intended as instruments of national policy, embrace a range of rather ambivalent goals, e.g., European technological development versus national economic growth, and basic research versus end-product development. Furthermore, the ECU may be pushing these consortia as vehicles, in part, for the development of proprietary technology when its large multinational companies would find closed alliances potentially more profitable. Recall that Siemens joined with IBM and Toshiba to develop a 256-megabit semiconductor, rather than pursue that objective through JESSI.[5]

Finally, consortia that are heavily funded by government are vulnerable to sharp budget cuts and shifts in public policy, national income, and political priorities.

As private-sector creations, R&D consortia emerge when economic incentives exist for some potential membership constituency. Mission statements reflecting such interests are likely to be focused and unambivalent. Also, consortia born of private-sector initiatives operate in a free market for research and development services. They survive and grow to the extent that they fulfill the needs of their member firms.

To conclude, *ongoing* R&D consortia are likely to be more effective as private-sector initiatives, funded in part by government when it is in the public interest to do so. The government-initiated and/or government-directed *ongoing* consortia noted in this study have had less success. On the other hand, there are numerous examples, both in the United States and abroad, of effective government-sponsored R&D consortia, *temporal* in nature and focused on achieving some particular technological objective.

CONSORTIA MANAGEMENT

Consortia formation, strategy, and management have been treated at length in preceding chapters; a reprise would serve little purpose. The following section, however, summarizes the author's conclusions about the key success factors in structuring and managing R&D consortia. They concern membership composition, R&D planning processes, the R&D product line, product delivery systems, and most important, leadership.

Membership

In ongoing collaborative ventures, membership cohesiveness on some significant mission greatly facilitates the formulation of a clear objective, the planning of the R&D agenda, and the structuring of revenue streams to fund operations. The broader the scope of the R&D program, the greater should be the similarity among potential consortium members in terms of their R&D needs and priorities. Attempting to accommodate a wide range of member subsets, each with different interests, is dysfunctional. To do so is to risk a loss in R&D scale economies and to invite continuing contention in prioritizing the R&D agenda. The narrower the mission, the more diverse may be the membership constituency, as long as each member finds the R&D program of value.

In ongoing consortia, vertical structuring adds to membership diversity and may exacerbate disagreements over R&D priorities and the allocation of funding. However, in vertically structured consortia that bring buyers and suppliers together for some specific R&D project, R&D objectives and funding arrangements are worked out a priori, avoiding much contention.

In defining the consortium's membership, the issue of exclusivity—that is, limiting membership to specific companies or to certain classes, such as domestic firms—may arise. When it does, it typically reflects a concern for competitive advantage and the containment of intellectual property within national boundaries or within the consortium. The effectiveness of exclusionary practices depends, however, on whether certain other conditions exist for maintaining the integrity of proprietary technology, specifically a small number of members and reliance on internal R&D resources. New technology that is developed through some supply infrastructure, as at EPRI, is quickly diffused and easily expropriated by excluded competitors, excluded classes of companies, and other free riders.

Membership cohesion on some clearly defined objective facilitates the resolution of issues that will inevitably arise with regard to the direction, strategy, funding, and R&D agenda of the consortium. At best, however, consortia members will differ in terms of their interests and priorities. To a great extent such differences may be accommodated by planning an R&D product line that serves a range of needs. Over the long term, the R&D interests and competitive posturing of members may well change. If so, an initially cohesive membership is likely to have greater success in negotiating new directions than one comprised at the outset of subsets with divergent interests.

R&D Planning

R&D planning is the soul of consortium strategy, and the most critical concern of its governance structure. Inputs to the planning process come from four sources: members, external constituencies, consortia personnel, and top governance bodies. R&D planning may produce less than optimal results if any one of these sources dominates the planning process, and imposes its will on the others.

Member inputs to R&D planning typically come through a committee or task force organization structured around R&D areas. It is usually set up to generate research proposals and review progress on existing projects. These operating committees, composed largely of member-firm representatives, are the consortium's vehicle for market research at the membership level.

Apart from the ideas it generates, the planning process is itself important. It may be the essential factor in creating a sense of ownership of the consortium's mission on the part of members. It provides a context for the exchange of information among members, and between member representatives and consortium personnel. Planning committees can also become a channel for the dissemination of technology.

Because R&D consortia often operate in the broader context of their industries, related technologies, societal concerns, and the national interest, it may be essential to tap the inputs of relevant external constituencies. EPRI's Advisory Council is an important contributor to the consortium's planning. Its thirty members represent constituencies such as consumer organizations, environmental and conservation groups, state and federal regulatory commissions, the scientific and academic communities, and utility equipment manufacturers. At SEMATECH and SRC, planning is based on the Roadmap, an industry plan developed in 1991 and updated in 1993 by more than a hundred representatives of the semiconductor industry, government agencies, and the academic community. The Roadmap spells out performance requirements to the year 2010 for manufacturing processes, equipment, and materials.

Both as task-force members and as program managers, consortia personnel have a working knowledge of their fields and are well positioned to sense opportunities for technological development. A case in point is the EPRI program manager who saw a possibility of breaking the stalemate in wind-power development that followed the lack of success with that mode of power generation in the early 1980s. His internal memo proposed the formation of a consortium of a small group of electric utilities, a major wind turbine manufacturer, and EPRI. What was needed, he said, was a sense of ownership on the part of the electric utilities. This program manager's initiative led to the successful development of wind power as an alternative form of electric power generation in the late 1980s and early 1990s.

Ultimately it falls to the consortium's senior governance bodies—usually a top-level research advisory committee and the board of directors—to structure the annual R&D plan. Their responsibility is to allocate funds across broad R&D domains in accordance with membership priorities, the interests of external constituencies, and the limits of anticipated revenues. Their particular contribution to the planning process is to ensure that programs adhere to the consortium's mission, and perhaps also to override bottom-up priorities in favor of some level of public-interest R&D and basic research in support of longer-term development.

Product Line and Product Delivery

Attracting and retaining consortium members may depend on offering a range of products in multiple forms disseminated through delivery systems designed to put new technology to work. Product forms may include solutions to operational problems, technical information, member-company personnel training, state-of-the-art equipment for member-company use, and marketable end products. Another dimension of product-line choice may come in the form of such membership options as subscribing to all or selected parts of the consortium's R&D program and offering customized R&D.

R&D product-line delivery is essentially a matter of marketing. To be effective, consortia marketing requires, first, a clear market segmentation scheme—that is, the classification of technology receptors in member firms according to their job-related interests. For this purpose, a market segment is some subset of the consortium's clientele who share specific needs for a consortium product. For example, SEMATECH differentiates between the technology information needs of managers of new semiconductor fabrication plants and the needs of those who are upgrading existing plants. Similarly, one may distinguish among member-firm technical personnel in terms of their job-related time horizons, to identify those more interested in basic research and those who find technology development more relevant to their work.[6]

A second requirement for effective marketing of a consortium's products is a system for identifying technology receptors in member-firm organizations. EPRI does this through its Technology Interest Profile (TIP) questionnaire, which may be mailed to hundreds of managers in each member utility. This allows EPRI to structure a market segmentation scheme based on application fields, such as distribution instrumentation and control, electric transportation, power-generation maintenance practices, and nuclear-plant corrosion control. Another approach might be to work through designated liaison personnel in member companies to identify technology receptors.

Third, because the marketing of new technology is the selling of change, an exceedingly important part of the process is reducing the risks of adopting new technology, and maximizing the rewards. Cost-sharing offers and showcase demonstrations may be used effectively to address the risks; opportunities for individual managers to improve performance measures and gain personal recognition help to maximize the rewards.

Success in R&D delivery may also be enhanced by cultivating and maintaining ongoing technology transfer channels within member companies. Of course, doing so will be easier when technological development is an ongoing process, rather than a series of one-time events directed at different receptors.

Finally, negative attitudes about the legitimacy of a marketing function in research organizations often inhibits effective technology diffusion. Nevertheless, the "We'll invent it, they'll take it away" attitude that characterized some consortia in their early years seems to be a thing of the past. The need to build technology delivery systems for moving new advances into practice is becoming more widely accepted.

Leadership

A case can be made that the requirements for consortium leadership are different from those of private-sector management. Consortia managers may deal with more demanding and diverse constituencies; their success calls for different qualifications. As for tasks, a founding CEO of an R&D consortium must often build a constituency among both potential members and external interests and also generate funding. Another critical task is turning the original vision into a clear, important, achievable mission. A consortium's leader must also attract highly competent technical personnel and able administrators. Finally, a consortium leader must establish governance structures and processes.

Robert Noyce (founding CEO at SEMATECH) and Chauncey Starr (founding CEO at EPRI) are examples of effective consortium leaders. Both had high recognition in their fields, strong technical backgrounds, and broad administrative experience. Both had a reputation for being even-handed in dealing with conflicting interests, held strong ideas about the consortium's mission, and professed a high level of commitment to its objectives. Their successors, Floyd Culler and Richard Balzhiser at EPRI and William Spencer at SEMATECH, responded to different priorities. However, all three paid close attention to the tasks of maintaining membership, assuring the support of external constituencies, and securing funding. Spencer introduced a more formal administrative structure, and established performance measures to document the returns member companies were realizing on their investments. Culler and Balzhiser built a complex and sophisticated technology delivery system.

These and other second- and third-generation consortia managers possessed broad administrative experience, including management of technology functions in the private sector and participation in senior-level industry and industry-government councils. While their predecessors may have dealt primarily with member-company CEOs, they themselves dealt largely with second-tier operating managers, who were more focused on the contributions the consortium might make to their firms' performance over the short term. This difference in managerial relationships may well account for the new emphasis on performance measures, delivery systems, cost control, and reduced risk levels in R&D planning.

Theory suggests that the quality of leadership in an R&D consortium may depend on the character of the core group. Two factors in particular are relevant. One is that the core group must be strongly committed, for both economic and competitive reasons, to the consortium's mission. The second is that it must identify with the broad national interest of the industry sector to which it belongs.

A PUBLIC-POLICY PERSPECTIVE

These lessons of managerial import have emerged from the experiences of R&D consortia in the United States, Europe, and Japan. What implications for public policy may be drawn from them? First, R&D consortia have contributed significantly to technological development and diffusion, national economic growth, and national competitiveness. They have had a positive effect on national levels of R&D investment. They have not dampened interfirm competition. For these reasons, collaborative R&D should be encouraged and supported as a matter of public policy.

R&D consortia have had particular success as creatures of the private-enterprise system. They have been less successful when they have been formed to carry out some overarching national policy, as they were in Europe. Furthermore, the one example in this study in which a regulatory agency assumed proactive oversight of a consortium—that is, of GRI—suggests that a consortium's interests might be better served without such intervention. Government influence may lead to mission ambivalence and the politicization of governance structures and processes.

To conclude, if consortia have the benefit of supportive government policy and strong management, they will continue to grow as economic institutions and to contribute to the advance of technology in their nations and the world. The conditions that brought about their formation in fields such as semiconductors, communications, and power generation must certainly obtain in other industries. These conditions include the need to develop and put new technology into practice; the existence of areas of noncompetitive R&D, in which corporations might agree to cooperate; and the availability of scale economies through R&D collaboration.

R&D Consortia:

A Member's Perspective

Decisions to form or to join a consortium seem often to be made in a crisis, influenced strongly by the call to action of respected industry or government visionaries. Concern for the long-run viability and sustainability of collaborative R&D ventures, however, should prompt potential members to make a more thoughtful assessment of the prospects for member benefits. This appendix offers a four-part framework for such assessments.

MISSION

- What is the mission? Has it been clearly conceived and articulated by the consortium's leadership?
- Is a consortium the best way to accomplish the proposed objectives, or would they be better pursued in a single-firm initiative?
- What type of consortium would best serve the intended purpose: open membership, exclusive, or closed? If closed, what firms should participate based on the complementarity of their contributions and competitive interests?
- Does the mission have the support of industry leadership groups and other stakeholders?
- Does the mission have a public purpose? If so, does it have public support?
- Is the mission achievable within the limits of proposed funding?

LEADERSHIP

- What is the composition of the core membership group? Does it include relevant industry leaders? What is the core group's stake in a successful outcome?

- What are the qualifications of the consortium's CEO? Can he or she build a substantial membership cohort, secure adequate funding, attract talented personnel, and gain the support of external constituencies?
- What other influences—for example, government funding or regulatory agencies—will affect the consortium's policies and shape its R&D agenda? Are those influences consistent with member interests or do they conflict?
- What are the interests of external stakeholders? How may they influence the direction of the consortium?

STRATEGY

- What is the membership composition? Does it have a common interest in the consortium's mission?
- How will the consortium's product line serve its members' R&D needs? The public purpose? Would the accessibility of the consortium's output to free riders significantly diminish the value of the consortium to its members?

Figure A.1   R&D Consortia: A Member's Perspective

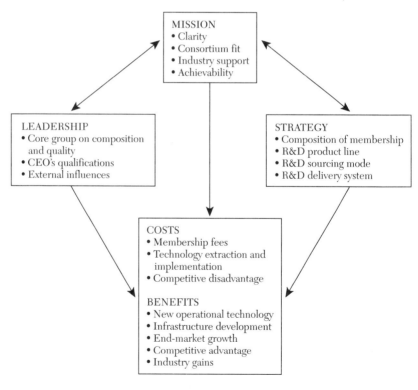

- Is the consortium's R&D sourcing mode consistent with its mission? How is the choice of a sourcing mode likely to shape the consortium's mission over the long run?
- Does or will the consortium have an R&D delivery system for moving its products into operational use expeditiously?

THE COST-BENEFIT EQUATION

- What costs is the individual member likely to incur in terms of annual payments, technology extraction and implementation expenditures, and the possible loss of proprietary knowledge and competitive advantage?
- What benefits may be realized in terms of new operational technologies, industry infrastructure development, and end-product market growth? Through the advancement of the industry's broad interests?

Mission, leadership, and strategy are interdependent; together they create member benefits (see figure A.1).

Notes

CHAPTER 1

1. VLSI Research, Inc., San Jose, Calif., 1992.

2. Semiconductor Industry Association, *Semiconductors: Foundation for America's Future,* March 1992, sec. A.

3. SEMATECH; VLSI Research, Inc.

4. SEMATECH's fourteen founding members were Advanced Micro Devices, American Telephone and Telegraph, Digital Equipment Corporation, Harris Corporation, Hewlett-Packard, Intel, IBM, LSI Logic, Micron Technology, Motorola, National Semiconductor, NCR, Rockwell International, and Texas Instruments. In 1992 three of the original members, Harris, Micron, and LSI, withdrew because of financial difficulties and a growing divergence between SEMATECH's research agenda and their immediate needs. The remaining eleven members represent 75 percent of the total domestic production of integrated circuits.

5. The Semiconductor Industry Association (SIA), formed in 1977, represents U.S.-based semiconductor manufacturers. As of 1995 it had sixty-five members. SIA's stated objectives are (1) to communicate U.S. semiconductor industry positions on matters of trade, technology, and economic policy to U.S. and foreign policy makers and (2) to develop unified responses to challenges facing the industry. Headquartered in San Jose, California, its committees deal with matters such as SIA's public policy positions, relevant legislative and legal developments, government procurement practices, occupational health, and environmental issues. SIA sponsors discussion forums and offers an array of publications on topics such as industry trade statistics, market forecasts, information technology, and public policy concerns.

6. G. C. Lodge and R. S. Williams, "SEMATECH: Innovation for America's Future" (Boston, Mass.: Harvard Business School, 1989), case study #9-389-057.

7. Ibid.

8. Interview, 16 March 1995.

9. Testimony before the congressional subcommittee on Commerce, Consumer Protection, and Competitiveness, 7 June 1987.

10. Interview, 16 March 1995.

11. *Chemical Week*, 14 September 1994, 13; Philip A. Palmer, Du Pont Specialty Chemicals, interview, 1 March 1995.

12. VLSI Research, Inc.

13. Interview, 6 February 1992, reported in *SRC 10th Anniversary Transcript,* 1992.

14. For a detailed discussion of industry standard-setting, see Martin Weiss and Carl Cargill, "Consortia in the Standards Development Process," *Journal of the American Society for Information Science* (September 1992): 559–565.

15. Interview, 3 February 1992, reported in *SRC 10th Anniversary Transcript,* 1992.

16. The twenty firms in the member group, all with sales in excess of $30 million, pay annual fees based on sales or purchases of semiconductors. The minimum fee is $65,000, the maximum, $3,054,320. SRC affiliates, all companies with less than $30 million in sales, pay $500 per million IC-related sales. The associates category was established to accommodate other R&D consortia and government agencies. SRC undertakes specific work for associate members on a contract basis.

17. Unless otherwise referenced, data on MCC through 1993 are drawn from David V. Gibson and Everett M. Rogers, *R&D Collaboration on Trial* (Boston, Mass.: Harvard Business School Press, 1994).

18. Shareholders paid a one-time fee of $250,000 plus an annual fee of $50,000 to become equity members and exercise MCC governance rights. They shared in any royalty income as well. Associate members paid an annual fee of $25,000. To qualify as a small business associate, with a $5,000 annual membership fee, a firm must have annual revenues of $20 million or less. Academic institutions may join as university affiliates for $2,500 a year.

19. Companies that participate in specific projects have exclusive and free access to the output, and may choose to license the technology to others, including MCC shareholders. Royalties from MCC-produced technology are divided three ways. One third goes to funders of the research, one third to support future research, and one third to MCC.

20. One hundred percent of the total kilowatt-hours (kwh) produced by the two government-owned utilities, the Tennessee Valley Authority and the Bonneville Power Administration, were represented in EPRI; 77 percent of the kilowatt-hours produced by investor-owned utilities; 43 percent of municipal-power kilowatt-hours; and 40 percent cooperative-produced kilowatt-hours.

21. Referred to here and in the press as "the RBOCs," "the operating companies," "Bellcore's owner-clients," "the shareholders," or "the Baby Bells."

CHAPTER 2

1. Speech by Joseph C. Swidler, chairman of the Federal Power Commission, to the Edison Electric Institute, 4 June 1963.

2. Speech by Joseph C. Swidler, chairman of the New York State Public Service Commission, to the Edison Electric Institute, San Diego, Calif., 7 June 1972.

3. Testimony of the Honorable George I. Bloom, chairman of NARUC's Ad Hoc Committee on Energy Research and Development, to the Senate's Committee on Commerce, 15–16 March 1972. Reported in *Proceedings of the NARUC 84th Annual Convention*, 993.

4. Interview, 1 October 1992.

5. Ibid.

6. This guideline remained in effect for the first decade. After that, review and approval processes were developed to give member representatives decision-making authority.

7. Interview, 1 October 1992.

8. Speech by Joseph C. Swidler, chairman of the New York State Public Service Commission, at a convention of the Edison Electric Institute, San Diego, Calif., 7 June 1972, 7. Confirming this point of view years later, Swidler wrote,

[The talk I made to EEI] contains a plea that EPRI should include in its program at least a modest laboratory component, a plea which went unheeded. My position was based on the experience of the Tennessee Valley Authority, where I labored for many years. Its own research, mainly on fertilizer and fertilizer equipment, was productive, while the work it farmed out, a relatively small amount, was not. Also it seemed to me that people with lab experience could better appraise the lab work of others. I had support for this position from the heads of prominent leaders in industry research. [From Swidler's letter to the author on 8 March 1995].

It is interesting to note that prior experience led Swidler and Starr to different conclusions with regard to sourcing policy, and that Starr's opinion prevailed. The outcome is consistent with Swidler's commitment that the Federal Power Commission would not interfere in EPRI's operations. As he said in the concluding paragraph of his speech to the EEI in 1963 (see note 1), "The FPC seeks no role in such an organization."

9. Op. cit., 1992 interview.

10. Data on MCC through 1993 are drawn from David V. Gibson and Everett M. Rogers, *R&D Collaboration on Trial* (Boston, Mass.: Harvard Business School Press, 1994).

11. *Electronic News*, 15 June 1981.

12. Ibid, 76–77.

13. Ibid., 198–199.

14. Ibid., 244.

15. Armstrong interview, 21 December 1993.

16. Gibson and Rogers, 218.

17. Interview with Dr. Craig Fields, 17 June 1993.

18. Ibid.

19. Ibid.

20. Interview, 3 May 1995. Dr. Dove was called back as chairman of the board of MCC in June 1994, after having resigned from that position in 1992. He served as CEO from 1987 to 1990.

21. Op. cit.

22. *Business Week,* 14 March 1994, 32.

23. Op. cit.

24. Op. cit.

25. Advanced Micro Devices, Control Data Corporation, Digital Equipment Corporation, Harris, Honeywell, Motorola, National Semiconductor, NCR, RCA, and Sperry. Mostek and Allied Signal joined in 1983, bringing the number of founding shareholders to twelve.

26. See Gibson and Rogers, chapter 5, 325–422.

27. *Business Week,* 8 January 1996, 32, 96, and 101.

28. *The New York Times,* 10 October 1994.

29. Excerpted from an interview with Mr. Larry Sumney. See chapter 1, page 6.

30. "History and Start-Up of GRI," GRI files, 24 March 1986, 3.

31. Dr. Linden's perceptions are that the so-called gas shortage had been artificially created by ill-advised actions taken by the Federal Power Commission under the Natural Gas Act of 1938 and the Supreme Court's Phillips Decision in 1954. Because of those actions, the field prices for gas interstate commerce were kept well below reserve replacement costs, leading to artificial shortages of interstate gas by the mid-1970s. Administrative actions by the Federal Power Commission and its successor agency, the Federal Energy Regulatory Commission, brought some relief. However, the eventual legislative relief, the Natural Gas Policy Act of 1978, created new problems by establishing significantly higher price ceilings for "new" gas, especially from depths greater than 15,000 feet and from "unconventional" sources, than for gas from existing reserves and more readily exploitable reservoirs. As a result, the supply of cheap "old" gas continued to decline, as producers concentrated on finding and developing reserves with the highest price ceilings to meet unrealistic projections of market demand. In the process, the efficiency of their drilling programs declined drastically. By the mid-1980s market forces finally overcame federal intervention, as consumers shifted from natural gas to other forms of energy, creating the long-lived gas "bubble." Interview, 17 September 1993.

32. "History and Start-up of GRI," 24 March 1986, 7.

33. Interview with Dr. Henry Linden, 17 September 1993.

34. Interview, 2 October 1992.

35. *Business Week,* 13 December 1993, 108.

CHAPTER 3

1. As of 1995, SRC's six science areas included microstructures, lithography, manufacturing processes, manufacturing systems, design, and packaging.

2. Interview, 26 May 1994. Dr. Fleming is director of external development in IBM's microelectronics division.

3. Interview, 13 June 1994. Dr. Skinner is director of the Fairchild Research Center of National Semiconductor Corporation.

4. Following are selected items from the Stipulation and Agreement Between the Federal Energy Regulatory Commission (FERC) and the Gas Research Institute (GRI):

1. GRI will use its best efforts, on a continuing basis, to achieve manufacturer co-funding, in those projects where such co-funding is feasible. For purposes of this Stipulation and Agreement, "project" is defined to be a collection of work elements or contracts aimed at achieving a single, stated R&D goal.

2. GRI is willing to accept a condition to the approval of its Application in this proceeding that its achievement of significant levels of reasonable manufacturer co-funding is an appropriate standard which may be used by the Commission in approving its Applications in future proceedings. . . .

4. GRI agrees to make the results of research conducted under its auspices available to the public through patent licenses at reasonable royalties and publications in accordance with Internal Revenue Service Regulations of the Internal Revenue Code; and, further, GRI agrees to apply all revenues received from patent licenses or other sales of technology and all revenues from the sale of assets or gas and/or by-products, together with interest accrued at commercial rates as credits against future annual budgets, as required by Paragraph 6.1.2(B) of GRI's Funding Formula and as required by Order NO. 566. GRI will undertake to achieve royalty income, to the greatest extent reasonable. . . .

6. GRI shall for this and all future annual programs and applications comply with the following:

    (1) Expenditures shall not exceed any project area budget by more than 10 percent of budgeted limits or $500,000, whichever is greater, at the project area level.

    (2) Expenditures shall not exceed any subprogram budget by more than 10 percent of budgeted limits or $500,000, whichever is greater, at the subprogram level for shifts between subprograms within a program area.

    (3) Limit the summation of individual project area reprogramming shifts in (1) or (2) above to 5 percent of the program's R&D contract research budget.

    (4) Document each project area shift which was made in the previous year's program, with a full explanation of what significant new information and/or other factors, such as DOE co-funding changes, etc., causes the reprogramming.

(5) Document each individual project sponsored in the previous year's program which was not funded, giving a detailed explanation of why the project was dropped.

(6) Document each individual new project funded with the previous year's program funds which was not included in the previous year's program, giving a detailed explanation of why the project was added.

(7) For all future annual programs, keep expenditures within budgeted limits for the designated program area unless appropriate reprogramming within the fixed program budget is authorized by the Commission in response to a written request from GRI. Any such request filed by GRI shall indicate in detail what factors necessitate and justify the reprogramming. . . .

[The above text is an amendment to Stipulation 6 originally approved by the commission in Opinion No. 96.]

8. In future applications GRI will assign priorities to projects and will use such assignments as guides for allocating funds; "an objective of future programming and funding shall be to move high priority new technology into use for the benefit of pipeline gas ratepayers in the shortest practical time."

9. Cost and benefit analyses will be prepared and considered in assigning priorities to projects and will be submitted to the Commission together with cost and benefit studies of certain ongoing projects. . . .

13. GRI will serve its future applications on all of its members and all state commissions, and there will be public notice with opportunity for comments. . . .

18. The officers of GRI will recommend to its Board of Directors to include five representatives of state regulatory commissions on its Advisory Council, one of whom will be chairman or vice chairman of its Advisory Council and will be invited to attend all board meetings.

5. Application of the Gas Research Institute for advance approval of its 1994–1998 RD&D program and jurisdictional rate adjustments necessary to fund the 1994 program, 43–46.

6. As of 1991, PGC's membership included Alcan Aluminum, Alcoa, American National Can, Armco Steel, Bethlehem Steel, Carpenter Technology, Cone Mills, Corning, Eaton Corporation, Ford, General Motors, LTV Steel, National Steel, Owens-Corning Fiberglass, Owen-Illinois, PPG, and Procter & Gamble. *Washington Representatives* (Washington, D.C.: Columbia Book Publishers, 1991), 798.

7. *Process Gas Company Group v. FERC*, 866 F2d 470 (D.C. Cir. 1989); *Process Gas Consumers Group v. FERC*, 930 F2d 926 (D.C. Cir. 1991).

8. At the same time PGC was pressing to bar GRI from research that might create new uses for natural gas, GRI had contracts with Ford and General Motors—both members of PGC—related to the development of natural gas vehicles.

9. 105 Stat. 531 (1991).

10. Specific cofunding percentages were mandated for end-use and gas-supply development, transport and storage of R&D hardware, and process development projects, as well as for different stages of project development.

11. Observations in this section are the author's alone. They do not represent the opinions of GRI's management or any of its constituencies, nor the author's interviews with GRI managers.

12. These negotiations resulted in a proposed funding formula, to take effect in 1993, which provided that approximately half the surcharge be based on the volumes of gas transported through interstate pipelines, and half on the demand/reservation component of the prices pipelines charged their customers. Previously, funding was calculated on volume only. In addition, the revised formula provided that for gas transported at discounted prices, the pipelines would deduct the discount from the surcharge obligation, up to the amount of the volumetric portion of the payment. It was also agreed that the funding formula would be reviewed no later than March 1, 1995, to determine whether it should be continued or revised, and that a "permanent" funding mechanism should be developed.

In addition to paying for gas delivered to the point of consumption or distribution, gas purchasers also pay to reserve throughput capacity on pipelines—all or some of which they might use, depending on seasonal demand. It is possible, then, to take account of both components of gas transportation charges—volume and demand—in establishing a formula for calculating the surcharge. The case for doing so is that while the pipelines would "write the check," probably both portions of the funding unit would pass through to gas buyers and on to consumers.

As might be expected, some LDCs (local distribution companies) and state groups opposed any recovery of GRI funding through a demand-based surcharge, believing it would shift the funding burden to the LDCs and their customers. On the other hand, gas producers wanted the funding unit to be based entirely on a demand/reservation metric. They argued that producers, not consumers, paid the surcharge when competing against alternate fuels like oil, because as a fixed cost, the surcharge was "netted" back to the producer. Gas buyers, they alleged, deducted the cost of transportation and other nongas costs to arrive at a price they were willing to pay for delivered gas.

In settling the issue, FERC concluded in its order of March 22, 1993, that:

> The 50/50 demand/commodity proposal is a hard-fought compromise among producers that wish to recover all of GRI's costs through the demand surcharge, LDCs that wish to recover all of GRI's costs through a volumetric surcharge, and GRI and the pipelines that seek to recover more costs through the demand surcharge to ensure GRI's funding. A purely volumetric surcharge would once again lead pipelines to resign from GRI and would not adequately ensure GRI funding. Further, other alternatives have been extensively discussed and reviewed at conferences and rejected by most of the parties. For these reasons the Commission finds that the 50/50 demand/commodity proposal is the best proposal to: (1) balance the costs of GRI among all classes of service, localities, pipelines, producers, and GRI; (2) spread GRI's funding as evenly as possible and over the broadest possible base of jurisdictional and nonjurisdictional natural gas services in this country; and (3) ensure that no one bears an unfairly disproportionate share of GRI's costs. Therefore, the Commission accepts the 50/50 demand/commodity proposal.

CHAPTER 4

1. Interview, 12 December 1993.

2. An Internal Revenue Code classification exempting from taxation certain organizations, including "business leagues," that are not organized for profit.

3. Advanced Technology Program: A Guide for Program Ideas, April 1994, 1.

4. Gibson and Rogers, 241.

5. Interview, 17 June 1993.

6. EPRINET is described in chapter 5.

7. See chapter 3.

CHAPTER 5

1. Gibson and Rogers, 325.

2. Interview, 13 June 1994.

3. Gibson and Rogers, 251.

4. Speech prepared in June 1992, not delivered.

5. Gibson and Rogers, 352–353.

6. Ibid., 340–350.

7. Interview, 26 May 1994.

8. Ibid.

9. Raymond W. Smilor and David V. Gibson, "Building a Technology Transfer Infrastructure," in *Technology Transfer in Consortia and Strategic Alliances,* ed. David V. Gibson and Raymond W. Smilor (Lanham, Md.: Rowman and Littlefield, 1992), 140.

10. Interview, 30 March 1994.

CHAPTER 6

1. Interview with Dr. Henry Linden, GRI's first president, 6 March 1995.

2. Gibson and Rogers, 56–57.

3. Jeremy Main, *Quality Wars: The Triumphs and Defeats of American Business* (New York: Free Press, 1994), 26.

4. Release, U.S. Department of Justice, P.L. 98-462, 11 December 1984.

5. In 1993 the provisions of the NCRA were extended to include joint production ventures, and the act was redesignated the National Cooperative Research and Production Act. Attorney General Dick Thornburg commented, "Antitrust uncertainty should not inhibit procompetitive [sic] joint ventures that would help U.S. firms succeed in global marketplaces. . . . Joint production ventures could promote the commercialization of new technology and help assure that U.S. leadership in basic research is translated into leadership in commerce as well."

6. *Business Week,* 27 July 1992, 59–60.

7. Interview, 26 May 1994.

8. Ibid.

9. Interview with Dr. John Armstrong, former vice president of research and director of science and technology at IBM, 21 December 1993.

10. Ibid.

11. Ibid.

12. *Business Week,* 27 July 1992, 59–60.

13. *Business Week,* 7 June 1993, 104–106.

14. "Sharing the Wealth: The National Labs and American Competitiveness," *Harvard Business School Bulletin* (February 1994): 36–41.

15. Interview, 23 March 1995.

16. This overview of government R&D sourcing through R&D consortia is based on the following interviews: Dr. Gary Denman, director, Advanced Projects Research Agency (ARPA), Department of Defense, 13 December 1994; Dr. Lance Glasser, director, Electronics Systems Technology Office, ARPA, 13 December 1994; Dr. Arati Prabhakar, director, National Institute of Standards and Technology, 14 November 1994; Dr. Joseph Bordogna, assistant director for engineering, National Science Foundation, 20 December 1994; Dr. Paul Robinson, director, lab development, Sandia National Labs, 15 December 1994; Dr. Ben Wilcox and Dr. Robert Crowe, DARPA, 23 February 1995; Mr. Zachary Lemnios, program manager, Microelectronics Technology Office, DARPA, 14 February 1995.

17. Gibson and Rogers, 13–15, 30.

18. Fumio Kodama, *Emerging Patterns of Innovation: Sources of Japan's Technological Edge* (Boston, Mass.: Harvard Business School Press, 1995), 165.

19. Howard E. Aldrich and Toshihiro Sasaki, "R&D Consortia in the United States and Japan," *Research Policy* (March 1995): 305.

20. Gibson and Rogers, 16.

21. Ibid., 38–43.

22. Ibid., 43–47.

23. Mariko Sakakibara, *Cooperative Research and Development: Theory and Evidence on Japanese Practice* (Ph.D. diss., Harvard University, 1994).

24. Ibid., 17.

25. Ibid., 138, 148.

26. "EU Policies in High Technology: Promotion, Trade or Protection," *Review of Business,* 22 June 1994, 18; "Cooperation: the Key to Survival in the New European Community," *Solid State Technology* (March 1993): 65.

27. "Shrieks Over Eureka—Research Is a Red-hot Issue," *Financial Times,* 17 March 1992, 101.

28. "Eureka, of the Technological Renaissance of Europe," *Washington Quarterly* (January 1987): 48.

29. "How Not to Catch Up," *Economist*, 9 January 1993, 93.

30. "A Mixed Report Card for Critical Technology Projects," *Science*, 18 June 1993, 31.

31. "EU Policies," *Review of Business*, 17.

32. "Esprit: Court of Auditors Attacks Programme Directions," *Tech Europe*, 4 March 1994, 2–3.

33. *Business Week*, 22 March 1993, 90–91.

34. "Eureka," *Washington Quarterly*, 48, 52.

35. *Tech Europe*, 11 July 1994.

36. "EU Policies," *Review of Business*, 17.

37. *Christian Science Monitor*, 25 August 1993, 88.

38. *Tech Europe*, 11 July 1994, 86.

39. Ibid., 85–86.

40. "Mixed Report Card," *Science*, 32.

41. *Business Week*, 22 March 1993, 90.

42. "Start-up No More: JESSI Gets Down to Business," *Electronic Business*, 18 May 1992, 67–68.

43. Ibid. "Talk About Your Dream Team," *Business Week*, 27 July 1992, 59–60.

44. "EU Policies," *Review of Business*, 18.

45. VLSI Research, Inc.

46. Semiconductor Industry Association, San Jose, Calif.

47. VLSI Research, Inc.

48. Ibid.

49. *Christian Science Monitor*, 25 August 1993, 88; *Science*, 18 June 1993, 31.

50. *Tech Europe*, 4 March 1994, 2–3; "Esprit D'Europe," *Unix World* (April 1993): 35–37.

51. *Business Week*, 22 March 1993, 90–91.

52. *Electronic Business*, 18 May 1992, 68.

53. *Financial Times*, 17 March 1992, 101.

54. *Business Week*, 22 March 1993, 90–91.

55. *Tech Europe*, 4 March 1994, 2–3; *UnixWorld* (April 1993): 36–37; *Financial Times*, 17 March 1992, 100–101.

56. "EU Policies," *Review of Business*, 18.

57. *Tech Europe*, 4 March 1994, 3.

CHAPTER 7

1. Russell Hardin, *Collective Action* (Baltimore, Md.: Johns Hopkins University Press, 1982), 20, 76; Mancur Olson, *The Logic of Collective Action: Public Goods and the Theory of Groups* (Cambridge, Mass.: Harvard University Press, 1971), 36; Mancur Olson, Jr., and Richard Zeckhauser, "An Economic Theory of Alliances," *Review of Economics and Statistics* (August 1966): 266–279.

2. Examples offered include group insurance, discounts on services, travel, and recreational programs and publications for group members. Hardin, 33; Olson, 61.

3. Olson, 22.

4. See in particular Robert Axelrod, *The Evolution of Cooperation* (New York: Basic Books, 1984); Hardin, 22 ff.; Paul A. Samuelson and William D. Nordhaus, *Economics*, 14th ed. (New York: McGraw-Hill, 1992), 209–210.

5. Axelrod, chapter 1.

6. Olson, 48.

7. David Hume, *A Treatise of Human Nature*, bk. 3, pt. 2, sec. 7, cited in Hardin, 40.

8. Hardin, 43, 45.

9. Mancur Olson, Jr., and Richard Zeckhauser, "An Economic Theory of Alliances," in Bruce M. Russett, ed., *Economic Theories of International Politics* (Chicago: Markham, 1968), 28, 39.

10. Olson, 34–36.

11. Olson, 33–34; Hardin, 20.

12. Sakakibara, *Cooperative Research and Development*, 17–19, 87–89, 95, 98, 115, 138–139, 148–149.

13. *Business Week*, 27 July 1992, 59–60.

14. *New York Times*, 28 January 1993.

15. Sakakibara, 146–147.

16. Hardin, 108; Olson, 62; Chester Barnard, *The Functions of the Executive* (Cambridge, Mass.: Harvard University Press, 1968), 146.

17. Olson, 43, 62; Axelrod, 20–21, 33.

18. Hardin, 38.

19. Olson, 36, 48; Hardin, 43.

20. Hardin, 43.

21. Hardin, 12.

22. Olson and Zeckhauser, "Economic Theory of Alliances," 27–28.

CHAPTER 8

1. See the quotation from Dr. Pallab Chatterjee, senior vice president and chief technical officer at Texas Instruments, in chapter 6, page 114.

2. Joseph L. Badaracco, Jr., *The Knowledge Link: How Firms Compete Through Strategic Alliances* (Boston, Mass.: Harvard Business School Press, 1991).

3. Mariko Sakakibara and Michael Porter also made this observation; see Sakakibara, 21.

4. Sakakibara, 151–152.

5. Chapter 6, page 125.

6. See the comments of Dr. Pallab Chatterjee and Dr. Daniel Fleming in chapter 5, page 100–101.

Index

About the Author

E. Raymond Corey is the Malcolm P. McNair Professor of Marketing, Emeritus, at the Harvard Business School. He joined the faculty in 1948 as an instructor in the first-year MBA course on Public Relationships and Responsibilities, and later developed the school's first course in industrial marketing. During his tenure at Harvard, Professor Corey has served as faculty chair for the Program for Management Development and the Advanced Management Program, director of Executive Education, director of Research, and faculty coordinator for the second-year field studies program.

Professor Corey has written numerous books on marketing including *The Development of Markets for New Materials, Industrial Marketing: Cases and Concepts, Marketing Organization: A Strategic Approach*, co-authored with Steven H. Star, and *Going to Market: Distribution Systems for Industrial Products*, co-authored with Frank V. Cespedes and V. Kasturi Rangan (HBS Press).